BATHROOM BOOK
of
FLORIDA
TRIVIA

Weird, Wacky and Wild

Michael Shaffer & Andrew Fleming

Illustrations by Peter Tyler & Roger Garcia

BLUE
BIKE
BOOKS

The Publisher: Blue Bike Books
www.bluebikebooks.com

Library and Archives Canada Cataloguing in Publication

Shaffer, Michael, 1974–
    Bathroom book of Florida trivia : weird, wacky and wild /
    Michael Shaffer and Andrew Fleming.

ISBN-13: 978-1-897278-24-6
ISBN-10: 1-897278-24-1

    1. Florida—Miscellanea. I. Fleming, Andrew, 1972– II. Title.

F311.6.S52 2007   975.9   C2007-902631-1

Project Director: Nicholle Carrière
Project Editor: Sheila Quinlan
Cover Image: Photos.com
Illustrations: Peter Tyler, Roger Garcia

We acknowledge the support of the Alberta Foundation for the Arts for our publishing program.

PC: P5

DEDICATIONS

To Mom and Dad, Lee and Jen, and the whole cast of characters that helped shape my Florida experiences, past, present and future.

—*Michael Shaffer*

ACKNOWLEDGMENTS

Thank you to the fine men and women toiling in our nation's bookstores, libraries, newsstands and wherever else you can peruse the printed word. And thank you to Al Gore and his compatriots for creating and developing the World Wide Web. Additional thanks to my friends and associates scattered throughout the world, especially the Atlantic Avenue Crew. And of course, a big shout-out to the great state of Florida, the real final frontier!

—*Michael Shaffer*

CONTENTS

INTRODUCTION

What is it about Florida? What is my attraction to this sun-drenched, sub-equatorial utopia? Time after time, I have traveled out of its borders only to feel a mysterious longing to return. (And no, it can't all be a case of Social Anxiety Disorder!) When the opportunity came up to write about Florida and to document its anecdotes, tall tales, urban legends, rumors and jaw-dropping realities, I jumped at the chance!

You see, when someone—usually a New Yorker—asks me where I'm from, I answer, "Florida, born and raised!" Almost always, this is greeted with a look of shock and disbelief, resulting in a strange mixture of contempt for the person asking and a sense of pride in myself. Why contempt? Well, think about it: with Florida's population growth putting the rest of the nation to shame, wouldn't anyone in their right mind expect a fair number of citizens to actually have been born in the state? And as for my sense of pride, I think native Floridians share a bond. We're a rare breed of modern-day pioneers taming the urban wilderness, knowing deep down that we thrive in one of the wildest, warmest, wettest and wackiest places in the Union. Yes, we're Americans, but we're also Floridians. You newcomers are welcome, but watch your step—you're on our turf now!

Not only am I a native, but I've also spent almost my entire life here, even my college years (as both a Seminole and a Gator). Various road trips with family and friends have taken me to almost every nook and cranny within driving distance. And in Florida, "driving distance" must be taken with a grain of salt—this state is big! The total area covers more than 58,000 square miles, and great stretches of that are indistinguishable from each other, just endless greenery as far as the eye can see interspersed with the occasional construction site. But once you do reach your destination, you'll definitely remember the experience!

Certain states, such as New York, New Jersey, Texas and California, have earned, whether willingly or not, a reputation. But Florida's reputation is still being made. A state so spread out has more difficulty in forming an identity. To this day, some Northern Floridians think very little of their Southern counter-parts, and more than a few residents have called for splitting the state in two! Northern Florida offers different plant life, (slightly) cooler weather, a generally slower pace, smaller towns and a larger percentage of Florida-born inhabitants (known as Crackers). Meanwhile, Southern Florida—the stereotypical image of the state for all those individuals stuck in snow—is generally thought of as more cosmopolitan, fast-paced, danger-ous and glitzy. Of course, these are just generalities, so calm down!

The state really came into in its own with the epic land boom of the late 1800s and early 1900s. Suddenly, a tidal wave of the hungriest, bravest, most charismatic, optimistic and forward-

thinking people, along with the criminals, con-artists, connivers, charlatans and crazies streamed into the state. Overcoming unimaginable obstacles, progress continued, and today, Florida is firmly entrenched in another, even more impressive explosion of growth and prosperity. And the only obstacle is the ocean itself!

So why do people continue to flock to, and stay put in, Florida? It can't all be because of the weather! For adventure, contemplation, financial and personal success, fame, true love, glamour or even a quick vacation, the Sunshine State is like no other place in America, and that's just the way we like it!

WHAT SETS FLORIDA APART

Yesterday, Arnold Schwarzenegger announced he would run for governor of California. The announcement was good news for Florida residents, who now live in the second flakiest state in the country.

–Conan O'Brien, August 2003

The Gulf State, the Peninsula State, the Orange State, the Everglades State, the Sunshine State—these are but a few of Florida's nicknames. But whatever you call it, it's truly an original, the wacky, weird, wicked and wonderful black sheep of the United States. Sticking way out in the ocean as if trying to make a desperate break, the entire state seems to be bursting at the edges. It's no wonder that environmentalists and developers alike worry about running out of unspoiled land in Florida.

Thousands of years ago, the area was home to various indigenous tribes, but the rude arrival of Europe's most adventurous, bloodthirsty and disease-ridden "discoverers" forever changed the population of what would eventually become Florida. Along with the European settlers, another Native presence made itself at home. Today's proud, political and prosperous Seminole Nation, one of the most successful tribes, only became what it was after the original people were killed or driven out. And the fall of one and the rise of another defines Florida perfectly: progress, momentum and success, at any cost!

The flags of five nations—Spain, France, England, the Confederacy and the United States—have cast their shadows on this sun-kissed patch of land, whether they were wanted or not. A seeming eternity of upheaval and turmoil, both natural and human-made, was inflicted on the region, leaving in its place a trail of dazzling cities, historical monuments, political dramas, legal battles and personal losses and victories. Florida is the home of the planet's leading center for galactic exploration and the nation's second biggest area for Sasquatch sightings (though we call him/her/it the Skunk Ape). Florida is the "it" scene for deal-making, people-watching and all-night partying! And we haven't forgotten about families and children of all ages; no other state boasts as many theme parks and tourist draws. Florida not only has Orlando, the world's amusement capital, but it is also the cradle of the circus industry, and it supports a thriving, year-round, beach-going public!

Virtually every sport is represented in the Sunshine State, and most of them—football, basketball, baseball, NASCAR (hello, Daytona!)—have done very well, thank you. Just this year, the University of Florida achieved an incredible goal by winning both the national football and basketball championships! This hot-weather state even boasts two hockey teams, one of which won the Stanley Cup. And of course, this is the nation's home for jai alai, a sport revered by the state's huge Hispanic population, which is itself a source of pride and political power.

Indeed, Florida has become the nation's real melting pot! The state's location, adjacent to one of the world's last Communist strongholds, has long generated both history and hysteria. But its location has also resulted in a population from all corners of the globe, along with their representative arts, entertainment, cuisine, tourism, economy, politics and education.

And sure, not all of Florida's past has been on the up-and-up, but that in itself made the state what it is today. Again, it might be Florida's geography—it does look like America's kickstand, after all—but it seems as though society's worst elements always end up down here. Since the state's earliest days, there has been a steady stream of conquerors, criminals, capitalists,

Communists, carpetbaggers and a multitude of scandal-ridden politicos. And many of these individuals met their end in Florida, such as Ted Bundy, Aileen Wuornos, Ma Barker's gang and even Al Capone. But the negative has been more than balanced out by the positive, and as you make your way around, you'll find no end to the good in this state. Welcome to Florida. Here's hoping you make it out alive!

OFFICIALLY SPEAKING

State Name

Florida was given its name by Spanish explorer Juan Ponce de León, who first landed on its sunny shores during the 1513 Easter season, known as *Pascua Florida* in Spanish, which translates as "Flowery Easter." While the Sunshine State is the most famous "Florida," other places that share the floral name can be found in Massachusetts, Missouri, New York, Colombia, Peru, Puerto Rico, Cuba, Argentina, Brazil, Uruguay, Chile and South Africa.

State Birthday

Florida joined the Union on March 3, 1845, as America's 27th state. It shares a birthday with inventor Alexander Graham Bell, Bulgaria, *Time* magazine, actresses Jean Harlow and Jessica Biel, heptathlete Jackie Joyner-Kersee and hip-hop pioneer Tone-Loc. Sixteen years later and wanting to hang onto its slaves, Florida seceded in order to become a founding member of the Confederate States. When that didn't work out so well, it rejoined the United States on June 25, 1868.

DID YOU KNOW?

Tallahassee was the only Confederate capital east of the Mississippi not captured by the Union during the Civil War!

State Capital

Located in the Panhandle, the capital, Tallahassee, is a Creek (also known as Muscogee) Indian term meaning either "old fields," "old town" or "abandoned village." Of course, the true meaning may differ among various members of the tribe. A growing metropolis, the city is also referred to as "Florida with a Southern accent."

Florida had been divided into the East and West Florida territories. Legend has it that when they were recombined into one state, travelers were sent from the previous capitals, St. Augustine and Pensacola. These travelers met in a back-woods spot, which was then chosen as the site of the new capital.

Tallahassee's estimated current population is 260,000. At one time or another, the city has been home to such notable citizens as Nobel Prize–winning scientists John Robert Stiffer and Sir Harold Kyoto, "Prime Minister of Funk" George Clinton, NASCAR driver Kim Crosby, "Famous Amos" chocolate-chip cookie founder Wally Amos, grunge-lite rockers Creed and socially conscious hip-hop duo Dead Prez. The city's most recognizable landmark is the Florida State Capitol building, a 22-story tower flanked by two hemispherical domes. It is so blatantly phallic it could make a nun blush.

Most official photos of the building are taken from the southwest or northwest in order to de-emphasize its Freudian features. Local legend has it that the Apalachee Parkway, the city's major east–west thoroughfare, was constructed to deny drivers and viewers a good spot to view the building head-on. In addition, the presence of some strategically planted trees helps to distract prying eyes. This architectural edifice has been the brunt of jokes for years, including boxer shorts with the silhouette of the building printed over the fly under the brand name "Legislative Briefs." A long-standing Tallahassee tall tale states that the original plans for the state building called for a fountain to be built in the center of the garden on top of the building.

State Seal
The original Florida government's mark of office was created in 1861 and was mandated to be "the size of the American silver dollar, having in the center thereof a view of the sun's rays over a high land in the distance, a cocoa tree, a steamboat on water, and an Indian female scattering flowers in the foreground." However, the design of the "Great Seal of the State of Florida" has changed considerably over the years. The mountains have been wisely removed (Florida doesn't have any mountains); the cocoa tree has been turned into a palm tree (cocoa trees aren't native to Florida); the steamer has become a sailboat; and the woman has had her headdress removed (only males wore headdresses), and her facial features changed from those of a Western Plains Native American to those of a Seminole. The sunshine, however, remains intact.

State Flag
The flag of Florida consists of a red diagonal cross on a white background with the seal of Florida superimposed over the center. For decades, the flag was simply the Florida seal on a solid white flag, but it was changed in 1900 after Governor Francis P. Fleming pointed out that it looked uncomfortably like the international white flag of surrender. Some people have complained that the cross is intended to pay tribute to the blue saltire (diagonal cross) of the rebel Confederate battle flag. However, there is no serious opposition in Florida to the current design of its flag.

DID YOU KNOW?

The term "Five flags over Florida" refers to the five different nations that have all claimed ownership of Florida over the years: Spain (1513–63, 1565–1763, 1784–1821), France (1564–65), Great Britain (1763–84), the Confederacy (1861–65) and the United States (1821–61, 1865–present). In addition, Fernandina was briefly under the control of a group of Mexican pirates.

State Motto
Over 80 percent of Floridians are Christian, so it should come as little surprise that the state motto is *In deo speramus*—In God We Trust. The pious paean is, of course, the same slogan of America itself (not to mention the name of spandex-sporting Christian heavy metal band Stryper's debut album). But, while lacking in originality, it certainly sounds better than "In Walt…" or "In Mickey We Trust." Despite Florida having been rocked by more hurricanes in recorded history than anywhere else on Earth, there has been no serious suggestion of changing its motto.

State Anthem

Way down upon the Swanee River,
Far, far away,
There's where my heart is turning ever,
There's where the old folks stay.
All up and down the whole creation,
Sadly I roam,
Still longing for the old plantation,
And for the old folks at home.
All the world is sad and dreary,
Ev'rywhere I roam;
Oh! loved ones, how my heart grows weary,
Far from the old folks at home…

–Stephen Foster, "Old Folks at Home"

Swan Song for "Swanee"?

The song "Old Folks at Home" was named Florida's official song long before the state became a popular retirement destination. But do you know the hidden story behind the song's selection? Also known as "Way Down Upon the Swanee River," the song was written by Stephen Foster in 1851 and tells of the supposed lament of a displaced slave who is desperate to return to the comforts of the cotton fields. But according to legend, Foster was unable to decide on the opening line's specific river. So, he left it blank and had his brother give some suggestions, such as Mississippi's Yazoo and the Carolinas' Pee Dee, which were both rejected. Then, they consulted an atlas and found the Suwannee River, which they promptly spelled incorrectly. Apparently, Foster never saw the Suwannee nor did he even set foot in Florida. Nevertheless, the song became a massive hit, kicking off a major flow of new tourists to see the river.

As the official state song of Florida since 1935, it has become a tradition for the tune to be performed as part of the inauguration ceremony for incoming governors, which is becoming increasingly awkward given the subject matter. Many feel that the song, written by a white Yankee songwriter attempting black vernacular, might be insensitive to African Americans. But in reality, Foster, an ardent supporter of the North in the Civil War, actually sympathized with the plight of the black men and women. And the song had its supporters in the black community, such as noted civil rights activist W.E.B. DuBois. Nevertheless, in 2007, Charlie Crist, the incoming governor, decided not to include it at his inauguration, as he felt it would be offensive to the state's African-American population. Crist instead went with "The Florida Song," which was written by jazz musician Charles Atkins, an African American as well as a Florida native. Atkins also wrote "Florida, My Florida," which was the official state song before "Old Folks at Home."

DID YOU KNOW?

"Old Folks at Home" inspired the hit songs "Swanee" by Al Jolson, "Swanee River Boogie" by Albert Ammons and "Swanee River Rock" by Ray Charles. The tune also received a mention in Irving Berlin's hit "Alexander's Ragtime Band," with the line: "If you want to hear the 'Swanee River' played in ragtime, come on and hear Alexander's Ragtime Band."

State Animal

Chosen after a statewide student vote in 1982, Florida's officially selected animal now teeters on the brink of extinction. The Florida panther (*Puma concolor coryi*) is a subspecies of mountain lion that lives in the state's ever-dwindling southern forests and swamps. Mountain lions, also known as cougars or pumas, once ranged throughout most parts of North America. Mistakenly perceived by settlers as a threat to humans, livestock and wild game animals, panthers were almost entirely eradicated east of the Rockies, and the surviving cats are now concentrated in rural pockets of Texas and Florida. As a result of their isolation, Florida panthers became genetically distinct from their western relatives and are now smaller, with longer legs and a broader skull. Protected from hunting since 1958, today there are only an estimated 50 to 70 panthers surviving in the wild.

DID YOU KNOW?

Panthers prey primarily on white-tailed deer, as well as on raccoons and other small mammals. There has never been a single recorded fatal panther attack on a human being.

State Bird

One of the Mother Nature's most impressive impersonators, the northern mockingbird (*Mimus polyglottos*) is able to imitate not only the songs of other bird species, but also a wide variety of other sounds, from cats' meows to car alarms. The mockingbird was adopted as Florida's state bird in 1927, a decision that was copied by Arkansas, Mississippi, Tennessee and Texas.

FABULOUS FLORIDA Male mockingbirds sing primarily to attract chicks. Although females sing as well, they do so less frequently, with less of a range and more softly than males do. Unmated males have repertoires of anywhere from 50 to 200 songs and, much to the annoyance of many Floridians, often sing through the night, especially during a full moon.

State Reptile

Of all of America's official state reptiles, Florida's is the only one known to occasionally dine on its citizens. The American alligator (*Alligator mississippiensis*), found only in the southeastern United States, is the largest type of alligator in the world and can weigh well over 1100 pounds. On average, alligators measure 13 to 14 feet long, though the largest alligator ever recorded in Florida was 17 feet, 5 inches long. The tail makes up half the alligator's length, and the animal uses its tail primarily for aquatic propulsion but also as a weapon of defense. Gators are capable of sprinting up to 30 miles per hour and have been known to attack panthers and bears. The name "alligator" comes from the Spanish *el lagarto*, meaning "lizard."

While there were only nine fatal gator attacks in the three decades before the new millennium, they've since killed 11 people as their natural habitat continues to disappear. In May 2006, three people were killed in just four days.

State Insect

Although Florida is better known for its windshield-splattering love bugs, ferocious fire ants and merciless mosquitoes, its official bug is actually the zebra longwing butterfly (*Heliconius charitonius*). Named the official insect in 1996 by Governor Lawton Chiles, the zebra longwing butterfly is common in South Florida, especially in Everglades National Park. Black with yellow stripes, the zebra longwing is unusual among butterflies in that in addition to sipping nectar, its diet also includes pollen, which contributes to a life span of up to three months—positively ancient by butterfly standards.

DID YOU KNOW?

Adult zebra longwing butterflies roost in groups of up to 70 and return to the same roost each evening, a rarity in the butterfly community.

State Marine Mammal

The West Indian manatee (*Trichechus manatus*) is one of Florida's most beloved beasts, but also one of its most endangered. Although nicknamed "sea cows," manatees are more closely related to elephants and are believed to have evolved from a wading, plant-eating animal. These gentle, slow-moving herbivores dwell close to shore in both saltwater and freshwater and can grow as long as 13 feet and weigh more than 3300 pounds. Despite their ungainly appearance, the blubbery behemoths are believed to be the basis of the mermaid myth.

Although they have no natural predators, manatees have been on the endangered species list since 1973, and it's estimated that only a few thousand are left in Florida's waters. One-third of manatee deaths are caused by humans as a result of boating accidents, pollution and flood-control gates that close automatically. The year 2006 is on record as being one of the deadliest ever for manatees, with a total of 416 deaths. Although experts believe manatees can live to 60 years or older, their slow development to sexual maturity and low birth rate do little to compensate for their tragically high mortality rate.

DID YOU KNOW?

Born on July 21, 1948, Snooty, the oldest manatee in captivity, resides at the South Florida Museum in Bradenton.

State Saltwater Mammal

Is it a porpoise or a dolphin? Even the Florida legislature couldn't quite decide and designated the "porpoise, also commonly known as the dolphin" as their official saltwater mammal in 1975. The two names are often used interchangeably, but the title is generally understood to apply to the highly intelligent bottlenose dolphin (*Tursiops truncates*), the species commonly found along Florida's coasts.

Florida's most famous dolphin was named Mitzi, though she is better known by her stage name, Flipper. The star of the early-1960s *Flipper* television series and movie, Mitzi was trained and filmed at what is now the Dolphin Research Center on Grassy Key. Although she performed most of the stunts herself, such as knocking guns out of the hands of bad guys with her tail or nose-butting sharks, a male stunt double named Mr. Gipper was the one who performed the famous tail-walking scenes. Mitzi died of a heart attack in 1972 and was buried beneath a 30-foot concrete statue in the research center's courtyard.

State Fish

Florida is the only state with two official fish: the largemouth bass (freshwater) and the Atlantic sailfish (saltwater).

Freshwater

Also known as the bigmouth bass or bucketmouth bass because, as you might expect, it has a very large mouth, the largemouth bass (*Micropterus salmoides*) is one of the most prized sporting fish in North America. Famous for always putting up a good fight for fishermen, the largemouth bass can be found as far north as Canada. It's also the state fish of Mississippi and of Georgia, where the largest recorded largemouth, at 22 pounds, 4 ounces, was landed.

DID YOU KNOW?

In the spring, female largemouth bass can lay up to one million eggs.

Saltwater

The Atlantic sailfish (*Istiophorus albicans*) is probably North America's most recognizable saltwater game fish and is the fastest fish in the ocean, with a recorded high speed of 68 miles per hour. The Atlantic sailfish takes its name from a dorsal fin that it can spread out like a sail. It usually keeps its "sail" folded down to the side, but when feeling threatened or excited, it will raise the fin to appear much larger than it actually is. Sailfish are 6 to 12 feet in length and can weigh more than 220 pounds.

DID YOU KNOW?

In 1934, author Ernest Hemingway caught a 9-foot, 1-inch sailfish in waters off Key West.

State Shell

The horse conch (*Pleuroploca gigantea*) is the largest snail in North America, and its shell can reach lengths of two feet. In fact, the shells are so roomy that their inhabitants can retreat entirely into them and remain there for months, if so desired. Young horse conchs have orange-colored shells, while adults have orange apertures.

 They say that if you put a conch shell to your ear, you're able to hear the ocean. This generally works best when the shell isn't inhabited.

State Tree

The sabal palm (*Sabal palmetto*) is the most widely distributed palm tree in Florida. Also the state tree of South Carolina (though it actually isn't a tree at all and is more closely related to grass), the hardy plant grows in almost any soil and has many uses. The durable trunks are sometimes used for wharf pilings, docks and poles. Brushes and brooms can be made from young leaves, and the large, fan-shaped leaves were used by the Seminole people to thatch roofs. It grows 50 to 70 feet tall, and its ribbed, fan-shaped leaves are five to eight feet long.

The sabal palm is also known as the cabbage palm, so named because the growing heart of its new fronds are edible and somewhat resemble actual cabbage heads. The buds may be roasted, boiled or even eaten raw. However, this practice is destructive because it kills the palm. The bud from which fronds sprout is the only point from which the palm can grow, and without it, the palm can't replace old leaves.

State Flower

The official flower of a state whose very name means "flowery" is, unsurprisingly, the orange blossom. The fragrant, white petals have long been associated with good luck and are commonly used in bridal bouquets and head wreaths. They are also used to squeeze out a citrus-scented version of rosewater. Orange blossom water is a common ingredient in Middle Eastern cuisine.

DID YOU KNOW?

Orange blossom honey comes from beehives placed in orange groves.

State Fruit

That the ubiquitous orange (*Citrus sinensis*) is Florida's official fruit is a no-brainer. Citrus is big business in the Sunshine State, bringing in an annual $9 billion and employing 90,000 people. The first orange seeds were brought to the New World by explorer Christopher Columbus. By the time Florida joined the Union, there were orange groves thriving as far north as St. Augustine.

The word "orange" comes from the Sanskrit *narang*, and the fruit first originated in Southeast Asia.

State Wildflower

Florida found itself with an official wildflower almost by accident. In 1963, the government purchased some sod from a farmer to use in a highway project near Tallahassee. It turned out that the sod came from a pasture that had been overseeded with crimson clover intended as winter forage for the farmer's cows. The Department of Transportation ended up receiving a huge amount of positive feedback from passing motorists about the unintended flower blossoms. The department decided to intentionally plant wildflowers along Florida's roadways, using mostly hardy varieties of native *Coreopsis*, also known as tickseed. The project has become so successful that the wildflower was officially recognized for beautification efforts in 1991.

Although easy on the eyes, tickseed petals usually have toothed tips. The name *Coreopsis* comes from the Greek word *koris*, the name for the equally toothy common bedbug.

State Soil

Myakka fine sand, a type of wet soil found only in Florida, was adopted on May 22, 1989, by Governor Bob Martinez as the official state soil. Myakka soil occurs in more than 1.5 million acres of flatwoods, making it the single most extensive soil in the state. The name comes from a Seminole word meaning "big waters."

State Stone

Florida's official stone is actually a fossil. Coral is made from the external skeletons of tiny ocean animals called polyps, which live in colonies attached to underwater surfaces. When alive, polyps combine their own carbon dioxide with the lime in warm seawater to form the limestone-like coral. Agatized coral, which was chosen in 1979 as the state's stone, occurs when silica in the ocean water hardens and replaces the limy corals with a form of quartz. This process, known as chalcedony, takes approximately 40 million years.

State Gem

Moonstone, a whitish variety of the mineral called feldspar, was adopted on May 20, 1970, as the official state gem. It was a bold decision given that moonstones, which are also the birthstone for the month of June, aren't actually found in Florida. Mind you, they aren't found on the moon either.

State Day

April 2 was designated by the 1953 legislature as State Day because that is believed to be when Ponce de León first set foot in Florida in 1513. As well as being International Children's Book Day, April 2 is also a holiday in Argentina (as *Día de Malvinas*, a day to honor their fallen soldiers from the Falklands War with England) and Iran (as *Sizdah be dar*, the last day of Persian New Year's celebrations).

State Nickname

The "Sunshine State" was only officially adopted as Florida's nickname by the state legislature in 1970, though the term had been appearing on license plates for decades. Florida has also been referred to over the centuries as the Peninsula State, the Orange State, the Everglades State, the Citrus State, the Flower State and the Gulf State. And after thousands of miscounted votes helped decide the 2000 presidential election in favor of George W. Bush, the governor of Florida's big brother, Florida has also become known as the "State of Indecision."

State Band

The St. John's River City Band was named Florida's official music group in 2000. Based in Jacksonville, the large ensemble has a variety of incarnations playing different styles, including big band, brass band, classical, swing and jazz. The band's ambitious aim is "to serve to the pinnacle of professional instrumental performance as an American art form, while enriching the lives of an ever-increasing audience." They have played at New York's Carnegie Hall and with such notable guest musicians as Chet Atkins, Dave Brubeck and Dizzy Gillespie.

State Play

Written by Pulitzer Prize–winning playwright Paul Green in 1965, *Cross and Sword* was declared Florida's official piece of theater by the legislature eight years later. The play, a reenactment of the founding of St. Augustine (only with more singing and dancing), was created to mark the city's 400th anniversary and ran every night but Sunday every summer for 40 years. Traditionally, the play had automatically received an annual stipend. However, rising production costs, theater renovations, shrinking tourism rates and changes to the state's funding rules meant less available cash on hand. As such, the producers were forced to apply for a state-sponsored arts grant in order for the show to go on. They were turned down, and the 1996 season was the show's last.

State Quarter

Minted in 2004, the Florida quarter features images that highlight the state's role in both the exploration of North America and outer space. Above the inscription "Gateway to Discovery," the coin features images of a Spanish galleon (representing the travels of such notable Spanish explorers as Juan Ponce de León and Hernando de Soto) and a NASA space shuttle (representing the travels of such notable American explorers as Neil Armstrong and John Glenn).

State Pie

It's not easy to find real key lime pie outside Florida. Once upon a time, key limes were commonly found in markets around the world, but they were eventually squeezed out by the more popular Persian limes and other varieties. Unlike other limes, key limes are a blotchy yellow rather than shiny green. They are also smaller, seedier and more sour, and they have the additional disadvantage of being difficult to pick because they grow on thorny trees. Key lime pie was declared Florida's official dessert on July 1, 2006.

Popular since the late 1800s, key lime pie is made with egg yolks and sweetened condensed milk baked in a graham cracker crust and usually topped with meringue. The dish first became associated with the Florida Keys because of the area's isolation. Before the Florida East Coast Railroad opened in 1912, fresh milk was hard to come by on the islands, and most residents made do with condensed milk instead. Because the juice of key limes is so sour, it instantly curdled the milk in a custard filling.

State Beverage

After handily squeezing out other possible local contenders such as Gatorade or the margarita, orange juice was named as Florida's official state beverage in 1967. Florida contributes approximately 70 percent of the nation's oranges, and an estimated 95 percent of the state's commercial orange production is made into juice at massive processing plants such as the Tropicana plant in Bradenton and the Minute Maid plant in Auburndale. Florida contributes an estimated 40 percent of the world's orange juice supply, and during the 2003–04 season, the state produced more than 1.5 billion gallons. The most popular type of juicing orange is the Valencia, but there are six other local, commercially grown varieties, including the pineapple orange, the honeybell and the Parson Brown. After Brazil, the United States is the world's second largest producer of orange juice.

DID YOU  KNOW?

Florida is famous for being the adopted home of yet another O.J. Former NFL star running back Orenthal James "O.J." Simpson moved to Miami in 1995 after a Los Angeles jury found him not guilty of murdering his wife, Nicole Brown Simpson, and her friend, Ronald Goldman. In 2001, Simpson was tried in Miami for burglary and battery after an alleged road rage incident involving a neighbor. "The Juice" faced a potential 16 years in prison, but a jury once again managed to find him innocent.

IT'S NOT THE HEAT, IT'S THE HUMIDITY

(Well, it's also the heat...)

Climate Range

The hottest temperature ever recorded in the state was on June 29, 1931, when the mercury topped out at 109°F in the Panhandle town of Monticello. The coldest temperature ever recorded in the state, –2°F, occurred in Tallahassee, just 25 miles away, on February 13, 1899.

Average January Temperature:
Florida Keys: 71°F
Florida Panhandle: 53°F

Average July Temperature:
Florida Keys: 84°F
Florida Panhandle 81°F

Bright, Sunshiny Days

Guinness World Records credits St. Petersburg with having the longest run of consecutive sunny days: 768 days, stretching from February 9, 1967, to March 17, 1969. For 76 years, from 1910 to 1986, the *St. Petersburg Evening Independent* donated free copies on any truly sunshine-deficient days. When the newspaper closed down shop for good in 1986, only 295 newspapers had been passed out, averaging less than four shady days per year!

A Snowball's Chance in Florida

The biggest snowfall in Florida history happened on January 19, 1977, when snow accumulated as far south as Homestead. Snow flurries also fell on Miami Beach that day for the first—and only—time in recorded history.

Rain Gain

Curiously, with an average rainfall of 53 inches, more precipitation falls on the Sunshine State than any other in the country, mainly because afternoon thunderstorms are so common from late spring until early fall. A sunny day may be interrupted with a downpour only to return to sunny conditions shortly after.

DID YOU  KNOW?

The phrase "cool as a cucumber" has its origins in Florida. On hot days, the pulp of a cucumber may be as much as 10°F cooler than the surrounding air.

Frightening Lightning

Although it is rarely trumpeted in tourism brochures, Florida is the lightning capital of the world. According to the U.S. National Weather Service, Florida sees an average of 10 lightning strikes per square mile each year, the result of its hot, humid summers and the state's location between two large bodies of seawater. The second leading weather-related cause of death in the country after floods, lightning zaps twice as many people in Florida than in any other state, a statistic attributable partly to the popular pastimes of golfing and boating. If you'd care to personally experience a lightning strike, go golfing on a Sunday in July between noon and 4:00 PM, when two-thirds of strikes occur. Sunday has 24 percent more lightning-related deaths than any other day.

The area of Central Florida stretching from Tampa to Titusville is known as Lightning Alley. Nationwide, the city with the highest rate of lightning strikes per capita is Clearwater.

Bolts and Volts

The average lightning bolt is only one inch in diameter but can carry as much as 100 million volts of electricity and be as hot as 50,000°F—five times hotter than the surface of the sun.

Lightning Strikes Advice

The 30/30 rule is a good way to tell if you're in danger during a thunderstorm. When you see lightning, count the seconds until you hear thunder. If it's 30 seconds or less, the storm is within six miles, and you should seek shelter indoors. Experts say you should wait a full 30 minutes after you hear the last clap of thunder before venturing out again. Lightning is unpredictable and can literally strike out of the blue up to 25 miles away from its parent storm. Other suggestions to avoid getting fried during a storm include immediately getting away from pools, lakes and other bodies of water; not using a tree as shelter; not standing near any tall objects; and keeping away from anything metal.

The Plywood State

Florida has two seasons: tourist season and hurricane season. The former tends to come during the winter months and the latter occurs from the beginning of June to the end of November. More hurricanes have made landfall in Florida than anywhere else in the world—a total of 58 have blasted the Sunshine State since 1900. They range in severity from a mild inconvenience to deadly. But the difference between losing your hat and losing your house can often be a matter of mere miles!

The Big One

A hurricane in 1926 referred to as the "Miami Hurricane," the "Great Miami Hurricane" or the "Big Blow" killed an estimated 400 people and left between 25,000 and 50,000 people homeless, primarily in the Miami area. People referred to it as the "Big One" until the "Okeechobee Hurricane," the first recorded storm to reach Category 5 status, hit two years later and killed over 2000 people. Exact numbers aren't known because most of the dead were migrant workers swept away after a storm surge from Lake Okeechobee breached the dike surrounding the lake and flooded an area covering hundreds of square miles. Most of the bodies were washed out into the Everglades and never found. In total, the hurricane killed at least 4078 people throughout the Caribbean and caused approximately $100 million in damage over the course of its path.

DID YOU KNOW?

Although it was founded in 1925, the University of Miami first opened its doors a few days after the Miami Hurricane passed. Many believe that the school chose the name of the Hurricanes for its sports teams to honor the memory of those lost to the catastrophe.

The Bigger One

The most violent hurricane in Florida's history hit on September 2, 1935. With Category 5 winds estimated to exceed 250 miles per hour (only an educated guess because all wind-measuring equipment was demolished), the hurricane killed a total of 423 people in the Keys. The majority of the casualties were World War I veterans who were building Highway 1, the 113-mile Overseas Highway linking the islands together. Those who weren't killed by an 18-foot wave that washed over the Keys were instead sandblasted to death. In 1937, a giant coral monument in their honor was built on Islamorada Key at mile marker 81.5. The monument, which also serves as a crypt containing their remains, was added to the U.S. National Register of Historic Places on March 16, 1995.

The Most Expensive One

If you count the damage in dollars instead of lives, Florida's costliest storm to date was Hurricane Andrew. Andrew struck in 1992 and devastated the Homestead and southern Miami-Dade areas with winds over 156 miles per hour, although an automated station reported gusts up to 200 miles per hour. The estimated cost was $26.5 billion in damage, and 23 people died. With a central pressure ranking as the fourth lowest in U.S. landfall records, Andrew remained the most devastating natural disaster in U.S. history until Hurricane Katrina came along in 2005 and destroyed New Orleans.

The Longest One

In 2004, four separate hurricanes—Charley, Frances, Ivan and Jeanne—tag-teamed Florida over a six-week period. Hurricanes Frances and Jeanne even pummeled the same area. The final toll was estimated to be anywhere from $29 billion to $41 billion in insured losses, tens of thousands of people made homeless and 125 dead.

Almighty Wind

Most of the billboards in the Orlando area were knocked down when Charley blew through town in August 2004. One particular billboard, however, not only remained standing but also had its most recent advertisement peeled back to reveal the following words underneath: "We need to talk. God."

It's easy to see how some people might be inclined to see four hurricanes in a two-month period as warnings or punishments from above, especially because of the role Floridians played in electing George W. Bush. A few years before, an ad agency in Fort Lauderdale handled an assignment to place a variety of billboards bearing non-denominational religious messages around the country—all signed "God." Seventeen different messages were used, including such wry decrees as "My way is the highway," "What part of 'Thou Shalt Not' didn't you understand?" and "Keep using My name in vain and I'll make rush hour longer." The "We need to talk" message was one of them.

Always Look on the Bright Side of Life

Florida may not have white Christmases, but we're learning to make do. Whoever came up with the following list, an email favorite in Florida, has helped make hurricane season a bit more bearable for countless residents.

Top 10 Reasons Hurricane Season in Florida is Like Christmas

10. Decorating the house (boarding up windows)
9. Dragging out boxes that haven't been used since last season (camping gear, flashlights)
8. Last-minute shopping in crowded stores
7. Regular TV shows pre-empted for "specials"
6. Family coming to stay with you
5. Family and friends calling from out of state
4. Buying food you don't normally buy…and in large quantities
3. Days off from work
2. Candles

And the number one reason hurricane season is like Christmas…

1. At some point, you know you're going to have a tree in your house.

WHERE THE WILD THINGS ARE

The Sunshine State teems with exotic creatures. Many, such as the official state creatures—the panther, mockingbird, manatee, dolphin and alligator—belong, while others, not so much. Florida's steamy swamps, murky waterways and luxurious tree canopies have become an unplanned paradise for all kinds of furry, scaly, clawed and/or fanged critters that have no business being there. More imported animals are flown to Miami than any other American city except New York and Los Angeles.

Breeders, dealers and owners of exotic pets are everywhere. But when pet lovers find their Komodo dragon has outstayed its welcome, or they move in with someone who doesn't want to share an apartment with an anteater, they tend to simply dump their former friend. Nature then takes its course with decidedly mixed results. Here are a few of the more colorful creatures, both alien and indigenous, that call Florida home.

MAMMAL MANIA

Bear Necessities

Florida is home to its very own type of bear. No, it's not some Disney drone dressed up as Baloo or Winnie the Pooh. All wild bears in the state are Florida black bears (*Ursus americanus floridanus*), the state's largest native land mammal and one of three distinct subspecies of the American black bear in the southeastern United States. Although all three are nearly identical, the Florida black bear can be distinguished by its narrower skull and by a white band of fur that sometimes appears on its chest. There are an estimated 1500 to 3000 Florida black bears concentrated primarily in the areas of the Ocala-Wekiva River Basin, Big Cypress National Preserve, Apalachicola National Forest, Osceola National Forest and Eglin Air Force Base. Although numbers are drastically declining because of loss of habitat, the U.S. Fish and Wildlife Service has not yet listed the Florida black bear under the Endangered Species Act as threatened or endangered.

Florida black bears are omnivores and eat mostly berries, acorns and fruits. They also eat insects, such as carpenter ants and termites, as well as the occasional armadillo, snake, raccoon, rabbit or white-tailed deer. But relax, tourists are rarely on the menu.

DID YOU KNOW?

Florida bears don't hibernate. Instead, from late December to March, they have a period called "wintering," when pregnant females give birth in the den and go without food. During wintering, males and non-pregnant females spend only a few weeks napping inside their own dens.

Bobcats

Unlike Florida panthers, their fellow members of the feline family, Florida bobcats are neither rare nor endangered. One of 12 subspecies of the bobcat, Florida bobcats (*Lynx rufus floridanus*) are found throughout the state. These nocturnal big cats usually sport coats that are pale brown to reddish with black spots. Bobcats are not picky when it comes to picking a den; they'll live in hollow logs, tree hollows or almost any opening in the ground. However, the open, grassy edges between flatwood and hardwood swamps offer good places for the solitary predators to stalk their prey, which is mostly rabbits, rats and ground-dwelling birds.

DID YOU KNOW?

Florida bobcats are generally about twice the size of house cats. Apart from bobcats being much smaller than panthers, an easy way to tell bobcats from panthers—in the unlikely event that you are lucky enough to see either in the wild—is that bobcats have stumpy or bobbed-looking tails (hence the name) and shaggy ear tufts and "sideburns."

"Deer" Prudence

You don't have pay to get into Disneyworld if you want to see Bambi. North America's smallest species of deer, the Key deer (*Odocoileus virginianus clavium*), can easily be found roaming wild in the Florida Keys. Relatives of the Virginia white-tailed deer, Key deer became isolated from the mainland thousands of years ago when rising sea levels cut off the islands. Looking more like medium-sized dogs than deer, "bucks" (adult males) usually weigh 50 to 75 pounds, and "does" (adult females) usually weigh 40 to 65 pounds.

Once hunted nearly to extinction, Key deer are still considered an endangered species. The National Key Deer Refuge, covering 84,000 acres (more than 131 square miles), was established on Big Pine Key in 1957 to help them recover. Their biggest threat comes from drivers on Highway 1, who kill between 30 and 40 deer each year, accounting for 70 percent of the total annual deaths. It is illegal to feed or pet Key deer.

Monkeys

Southern Florida has more wild monkeys than you could shake a stick at, not that shaking sticks at wild monkeys is a wise idea! These primates come in all shapes, sizes and dispositions and from various backgrounds. Some are the descendants of extras used in the *Tarzan* movies filmed in the 1930s, others are former guinea pigs of the Charles River Laboratories in the Keys, and still others are escapees from failed tourist attractions or misguided pet owners. Among the larger colonies are the African vervet monkeys in Broward County and Fort Lauderdale, and the rhesus macaques around Ocala and on an island near Homosassa.

Opossums

Florida's only marsupial—and member of the planet's oldest surviving mammal family—is the Virginia opossum (*Didelphis virginiana*). About the size of a house cat, opossums hang out throughout the state in virtually all habitats. They are highly intelligent for animals with such small brains, and they have thumbs on their hind feet that they use adeptly to infiltrate all but the most high-tech of garbage can lids. When threatened, they tend to go limp and pretend to be dead, hence the term "playing possum." Oh, and the names "possum" and "opossum" are interchangeable.

Paying Possum Tribute

In 1982, the Florida legislature passed a joint resolution proclaiming the first Saturday in August as Possum Day. Unlike Groundhog Day, Possum Day is unrelated to any innate ability of the nocturnal marsupial to help forecast the weather (which, in Florida, is generally either sunny or hurricane-rich). Instead, possums get the honor because they are a reliable source of food when the going gets tough. As a monument erected in the possums' honor puts it: "Their presence has provided a source of nutritious and flavorful food in normal times and has been important aid to human survival in times of distress and critical need." And if that's not enough possum partying, head to Wausau, the self-proclaimed "Possum Capital of the U.S." On the first Saturday in August, this Panhandle town celebrates the Annual Possum Festival and Fun Day.

FOR THE BIRDS

Fowl Fray

Although chickens are hardly anyone's idea of a unique or exotic species, Florida is probably the only place in the world where they have the run of an entire city. Key West's chickens (*Gallus gallus domesticus*) give new meaning to the term "free-range." The island's chicken history goes back to the mid-1800s, when birds were kept for food and cockfights. Over the years, the chickens were released or escaped, and the population quickly took off on the two-by-four-mile island. Now too numerous to count, they've become a plucky, unofficial symbol of Key West's laid-back lifestyle.

And on that island, there are two kinds of people: those who are pro-chicken and those who are not. The people who like them point out that the chickens perform a valuable service by amusing tourists and eating scorpions, ticks, cockroaches, termites, snails and other pests. Those people who don't like them claim that the chickens *are* pests who tear up yards, cause accidents, wake up residents early in the morning, "do their business" everywhere and shoot dirty looks at patrons leaving the southern city's sole KFC outlet.

In 2004, the city hired a chicken catcher to trap birds and take them to a mainland farm. However, upset residents sabotaged the effort by freeing and feeding the chickens. The chicken catcher and the city eventually parted ways after he had collected a little over 500 birds.

Flamingos

Even though the vast majority of birds that live on the Eastern Seaboard spend their winters in Florida, there is no bird as closely identified with the state as the flamingo. And this is a bit odd considering that the bird isn't actually native to Florida. Nearly everyone knows what flamingos look like—pink birds with long legs. You can see them at just about every zoo. You can find them in storybooks. Alice uses flamingos as croquet mallets in *Through the Looking Glass*.

The type of pink flamingo found in Florida is known as the Caribbean flamingo (*Phoenicopterus ruber ruber*). This species traditionally breeds only in South America, Mexico's Yucatán Peninsula and the islands of the northern Caribbean. Most sightings in southern Florida are usually escapees from captivity, though as natives and tourists are aware, flamingos do frequent the state's theme parks and sanctuaries. Additionally, many of these flamingos may be Cuban refugees, and at least one bird banded as a chick in the Yucatán Peninsula has been sighted in

Everglades National Park. Flamingos prefer salty lagoons, mud-flats and shallow, brackish coastal or inland lakes. Their distinctive pink coloring comes from all the shrimp they eat. The more they eat, the pinker they become, though zoos have been known to help the process along by putting dye in the birds' food. Baby flamingos are usually gray or white.

DID YOU KNOW?

In November 2006, the plastic pink flamingo went the way of the dodo. Or more accurately, it stopped reproducing. Union Products, maker of the durable icons of lawn decoration, finally shut down the factory that made them just two months shy of its 50th birthday, citing the rising cost of plastic resins and declining interest in lawn kitsch.

MILES AND MILES OF RAMBUNCTIOUS REPTILES

Prehistoric Creatures

In the face of overwhelming evidence, the extinction of the dinosaurs in Florida may not be definite. From 1955 to 1961, witnesses in the Jacksonville area reported sightings of giant creatures in the St. Johns River. Reports stated that the creatures resembled a brontosaurus or an enormous manatee, with gray, leathery, elephant-like skin. The creatures were said to come ashore and graze on plants, leaving a wide, mashed-down trail in their wake. Interestingly, the sightings centered around the Blue Springs area, a prime manatee habitat.

In 1975, pleasure boaters on the St. Johns River near Jacksonville claimed to spot a dragon-like creature emerging from and then disappearing back into the deep water. Allegedly, the dragon sported a head like a giant snail, complete with two horns. The creature also made an earlier appearance in 1962, when some scuba divers near Pensacola reported being attacked by the creature. The creature was said to have tipped over the divers' small boat, killing all but one of the men. The surviving diver claimed that the creature had a long, rigid, 10-foot-long neck, and a head with small eyes and a wide mouth that it whipped around like a snake.

Snakes Alive!

Although 45 species of snakes are found in Florida, only six are venomous. The first four are members of the Crotalidae family, otherwise known as pit vipers, which inject poison that destroys the walls of blood vessels. The fifth is from the Elapidae family, known instead for producing venom that paralyzes its prey, thereby allowing it to be nibbled at the snake's leisure. The sixth, the Burmese python, a member of the Boidae family, is actually only a Florida resident because of careless owners who have released them into the wild. Unpleasant encounters with all six, however, are rare.

The Eastern Diamondback Rattlesnake

The largest and deadliest of the pit vipers, the diamondback rattlesnake (*Crotalus adamanteus*), is usually between three and six feet long. Its body is dark or light brown with a distinctive row of large diamond shapes edged in yellow running down the length of its back. Although it's commonly thought that the diamondback conveniently alerts its victims with a rattle before attacking, researchers have found that this may not be true. The snake has actually been observed stalking its prey with no sound or movement before suddenly striking.

Diamondbacks prey on rats, mice and other small animals often considered pests, but most Floridians are so scared of them that they generally kill the snakes on sight. Combined with habitat loss and commercial hunting for their skins, needless killing out of fear has caused their numbers to seriously decline, though the species is not yet considered endangered.

 The largest specimens of the eastern diamondback ever recorded were, respectively, 8 feet, 10 inches and 8 feet, 5 inches long. Both were found in Florida.

The Pygmy Rattlesnake

As the name implies, pygmies are smaller than most other types of rattlesnakes. Usually only 12 to 24 inches long, the pygmy rattlesnake (*Sistrurus miliarius barbouri*) is grayish brown with reddish markings. The pygmy always rattles before striking and its bites aren't fatal, but the rattle can be hard to hear. It is an aggressive biter, and the bites are extremely painful.

The Cottonmouth

Also known as the water moccasin, the cottonmouth (*Agkistrodon piscivorous conanti*) got its name from the white insides of its mouth and its habit of opening its mouth wide and hissing when threatened. This habit gave the snake a somewhat unde-served reputation for being aggressive. The olive green to brown snake usually measures 20 to 48 inches long and has a heavy body ending in a thin tail. The cottonmouth is rarely found far from a permanent water source.

DID YOU KNOW?

Some people mistakenly believe that cottonmouths lie in wait on tree limbs overhanging water so they can drop into boats and attack. What actually happens is that similar-looking but harm-less brown water snakes often bask on tree limbs over the water, and when frightened by approaching objects, they tend to try to escape by throwing themselves into the water. Occasionally, they miss and fall into a boat instead and are usually beaten to death for looking too much like a poisonous snake.

The Copperhead

Often mistaken for a cottonmouth, the copperhead (*Agkistrodon contortrix contortrix*) is only found in the Florida Panhandle. Adults usually measure 22 to 36 inches long and are grayish brown with dark brown bands, though they may have an overall pinkish tint. Copperheads have an hourglass-shaped head with a deep facial pit between the nostril and the eye. They aren't usually very aggressive nor are their bites fatal.

The Eastern Coral Snake

A relative of the cobra, the coral snake is small but deadly; its venom is the deadliest in North America. But at least it's pretty to look at. The body of a coral snake (*Micrurus fulvius fulvius*) is ringed with black, yellow and red stripes and, from the snout to the eyes, the head is black. Adult coral snakes usually measure between 20 and 30 inches long. These snakes are often confused with harmless scarlet king snakes, which have similar colorful markings. A handy trick to help you tell them apart is the rhyme "If red touches yellow, it can kill a fellow. If red touches black, venom lack." The phrase "If its nose is black, it's bad for Jack," has also been substituted on occasion. Coral snakes are not particularly aggressive and account for less than one percent of the number of snakebites in the U.S. each year.

DID YOU KNOW?

Coral snakes are elapids, venomous snakes found in tropical and subtropical regions. They are characterized by a set of hollow, fixed fangs through which they inject venom. Because of the time it takes for the venom kick in, coral snakes have a habit of holding onto a victim when biting, unlike pit vipers, which have retractable fangs and tend to prefer to strike and let go immediately.

The Canebrake Rattlesnake

Also known as the timber rattlesnake, this snake (*Crotalus horridus atricaudatus*) adorned the flags on board the first Continental Navy's ships during the American Revolution. Adult canebrake rattlesnakes average 36 to 60 inches long, though the record is 74.5 inches. Pinkish gray or tan in color, these snakes sport reddish brown stripes, large, black, chevron-like crossbands on their backs and uniformly black tails.

They have large heads and may have dark, diagonal lines running through or just behind the eye, as well as catlike pupils. Canebrake rattlesnakes also have a facial pit between their eyes and nostrils.

Burmese Pythons

One of the biggest examples, literally, of a species that has no business inhabiting Florida's ecosystem is the fearsome Burmese python. Capable of growing more than 20 feet long in its natural Southeast Asian habitat, the Burmese python (*Python molurus bivittatus*) is one of the largest snakes in the world and an inexplicably popular pet in America. Over the last 20 years, unwanted pythons have begun to overrun the Everglades; local wildlife officials have pulled several hundred of them out of the park in the past few decades because the snakes are beginning to give alligators a run for their money as the area's apex predator.

Gator Ate

On October 5, 2005, near Miami, researchers with the South Florida Natural Resources Center made the gruesome discovery of the carcass of a 13-foot Burmese python. Apparently the python had died while trying to swallow a 6-foot alligator; witnesses found the alligator's hindquarters protruding from the snake's shredded midsection. They speculated that as the alligator was being partially digested, it had tried to claw at the python's stomach. On three previous occasions, alligators had won, or at least tied, when competing against pythons. But biologists fear that non-native snakes, such as pythons, may soon wipe out native species in the Everglades. Over the past two years, an estimated 150 pythons have been captured in the area.

Crack is Wack (in a Gator Attack)!

In November 2006, police responding to an emergency at Lake Parker just outside Lakeland were shocked to find Adrian Apgar, 45, slumped over in an alligator's jaws in chest-deep water. The officers dove into the water and tried to wrench Apgar's arm from the gator's mouth. In all, it took three deputies and their sergeant 20 minutes of exhausting tug-of-war with the gator before they managed to rescue Apgar and carry him to shore. Apgar revealed that he'd been smoking crack cocaine and had fallen asleep on the shore, where he'd been attacked by the alligator. Apgar underwent surgery for his injuries, which included a nearly severed left arm, a broken right arm and bites to his buttocks and leg. Later, an 11-foot, 9-inch, 600-pound alligator—thought to be the one that attacked Apgar—was trapped and killed by state wildlife authorities. According to the Florida Fish and Wildlife Conservation Commission, the alligator had to be euthanized to protect the public.

DID YOU KNOW?

The urban legend of alligators living in the sewers of New York City has a possible Florida explanation. In the late 1930s, West Palm Beach mayor Ted Brown mailed two baby alligators as gifts for the postmaster general and the mayor of New York to celebrate the opening of the town's airport. The gators were last seen boarding a plane headed north.

What a Croc!

Florida doesn't have nearly as many crocodiles as it does alligators. Now considered an endangered species, there are only a few hundred or so American crocodiles (*Crocodylus acutus*) left in the country, primarily in the southern Everglades and Key Largo area. They prefer brackish coastal waters and can be distinguished from gators by their snouts, which are longer and more V-shaped, and also by a fourth tooth that is visible when their mouths are closed. The crocodile gets its name from the Greek *krokodilos*, a compound word from *kroke* (stone) and *dilos* (worm), a name that reflects crocs' habit of basking in the sun on rocky banks of the Nile River. Although known to grow to nearly 15 feet long, American crocodiles are shy, avoiding contact with humans whenever possible. No fatal attack on a human by a croc has ever been recorded in Florida, which you certainly can't say for alligators.

Nile Monitor Lizards

Cape Coral is the state's fastest growing city, but not all new residents are human. Dagger-clawed, blue-tongued and up to seven feet long, Nile monitor lizards have established more than just a scaly toehold in the city, the second most sprawling city in the state after Jacksonville. Nile monitor lizards (*Varanus niloticus*) are native to Africa, where they rank as the continent's largest lizard, but you can buy them in pet stores throughout Florida without even needing a permit. There are now approximately

1000 of the giant lizards living free in the area, most likely the result of a breeding pair or a pregnant female having escaped from or been released by a pet owner.

Residents now find the lizards in their swimming pools, on their roofs, sunning on their sea walls and devouring their cats. The city's combination of large areas of water, woods and undeveloped land that can be easily dug up is a Nile monitor's idea of paradise. Although they eat everything from roadkill to smaller fellow lizards, their favorite food is eggs: birds' eggs, snakes' eggs, even crocodiles' eggs. Unfortunately, Cape Coral also has (for now) Florida's densest population of burrowing owls, who, as their name suggests, lay their eggs in small burrows, making for a veritable Nile monitor buffet.

Sea Turtle Trivia

Five different species of endangered sea turtles are currently found in Florida: green, loggerhead, leatherback, hawksbill and Kemp's ridley. All five are protected under state and federal laws.

The Loggerhead

Florida's most common sea turtle is named for its great big head. Its powerful jaws allow it to easily crush the clams, crabs and other armored animals it prefers to dine on. The loggerhead (*Caretta caretta*) is among the larger sea turtles; an adult weighs an average of 275 pounds and has a shell length of about three feet. A slow swimmer even by turtle standards, the loggerhead occasionally falls prey to sharks, and a loggerhead missing a flipper or a chunk of its shell is a fairly common sight. The turtle compensates for its lack of speed with endurance. One turtle that had been tagged at Melbourne Beach, for example, was captured off the coast of Cuba 11 days later.

The Green Turtle

More streamlined than the lumbering loggerhead, the green turtle (*Chelonia mydas*) weighs an average of 350 pounds. It gets its name from its interior rather than its exterior. Green turtles have the misfortune of being quite tasty and were highly prized by early European settlers for their green-tinted, fatty meat, the result of their algae-heavy diets. After merchants figured out that the turtles could be kept alive by turning them on their backs in the shade, they began shipping them back to the Old World en masse. By 1878, 15,000 green turtles a year were shipped from Florida to England. Teetering on the brink of extinction, there are now 100 to 1000 green turtles nesting near Indian River Lagoon, the Florida Keys, Homosassa, Crystal River and Cedar Key from June through September.

The Leatherback

Much larger and capable of diving deeper, traveling farther and surviving in colder waters, the leatherback (*Dermochelys coriacea*) is a one-of-a-kind turtle. Usually weighing from 500 to 1500 pounds, its shell is made from a tough, leathery skin (hence the name) rather than the usual scales. This turtle is usually black with white, pink and blue splotches and has no claws on its flippers. Leatherbacks eat soft-bodied animals, especially jellyfish, and their throats and jaws are lined with stiff spines that aid in swallowing their goopy prey. They are capable of descending more than 3000 feet deep and of traveling more than 3000 miles from their nesting beaches. An estimated 30 to 60 of these turtles nest in Florida.

The Hawksbill

While green turtles nearly disappeared because they were over-hunted for their meat, the hawksbill's biggest liability is its beautiful shell. Shaded with black and brown markings on a background of amber, these shells are still in demand on the black market to make jewelry, hair decorations and other ornaments. Weighing 100 to 200 pounds, hawksbills *(Eretmochelys imbricata)* got their name because of their bird-like beaks. Hawksbills are unique in that they feed primarily on sponges. Although sponges are composed of thin, glasslike needles, they don't seem to bother the turtles. Hawksbills are the most tropical of the sea turtles and are frequently spotted off the Florida Keys.

The Kemp's Ridley

Both the rarest and most endangered sea turtle in the world, the Kemp's ridley *(Lepidochelys kempii)* is truly unique in that it has only one major nesting beach. This mysterious enclave in the Gulf of Mexico, known as Rancho Nuevo, was unknown until 1947, when a Mexican engineer made a film depicting 40,000 Kemp's ridleys crawling ashore in broad daylight to lay their eggs. But time has not been kind to these turtles; there are fewer than 1000 nesting females left worldwide. These turtles have a reputation for toughness, yet they are smaller than other species, weighing only 85 to 100 pounds and measuring 24 to 32 inches in shell length. The Kemp's ridley's diet consists chiefly of crabs and other crustaceans.

OUR FISHY FRIENDS

The Shark Bait Capital of America

More than half of the world's shark attacks take place in the waters off the coast of Florida. There have been 544 recorded shark attacks and 13 fatalities in the state since people first began counting in 1882, and numbers have shot up enormously over the past few decades. Since 1990, there have been an average of 21 attacks a year, but this number is more a reflection of Florida's rapidly increasing population than any new aggressiveness from the sharks. If you're wondering which are the safest beaches, the International Shark Attack Files (ISAF), based at the University of Florida, has a website that provides helpful statistics and maps on shark attacks around the world and also a detailed map of Florida showing where the most and fewest attacks have occurred.

Apart from staying out the ocean, here a few other things you can do to cut down the odds of being attacked:

1. Always swim in a group; sharks usually go for single individuals. If you are swimming with only one other person, try to make sure you can swim faster than him/her.

2. Avoid swimming in the dark; sharks are most active at night and are, obviously, harder to see.

3. Don't go in the water if you're bleeding; a shark can detect a single drop of blood in a million drops of water (25 gallons) and can smell blood a quarter of a mile away.

4. Avoid brightly colored clothing and uneven, murky water; sharks see contrast particularly well.

5. Don't wear shiny jewelry; the reflected light can look like tempting, shiny fish scales.

6. Avoid water containing sewage; it attracts fish, which in turn attract sharks.

7. Try not to splash a lot.

8. Avoid sandbars or steep drop-offs; these are popular hang-outs for sharks.

9. Don't think that just because dolphins are nearby, sharks aren't; both eat the same foods—apart from us, that is.

10. Get out of the water immediately if you hear a tuba playing the "Dum-dum, dum-dum, dum-dum-dum-dum" theme from the movie *Jaws*. Better safe than sorry!

The B-52s' Favorite Crustacean

Although not held in as high international esteem as their crustacean contemporaries off the coast of Maine, spiny lobsters (*Panulirus argus*) nonetheless provide Florida's largest commercial fishery. The commercial harvest, which runs from August through March, pulls in around six million pounds per season, with an average annual value of over $20 million.

Also known as rock lobsters, crawfish, crayfish or simply "bugs," spiny lobsters are different from true lobsters in that they don't have any claws with which to defend themselves. Instead, they must make do with waving long antennae linked over their eyes to scare off predators. Spiny lobsters get their name from the spiky spines that cover their bodies. They vary in color from off-white to dark red-orange and are found almost exclusively in the waters surrounding the Florida Keys.

DID YOU KNOW?

Each year, the recreational lobster season runs for two days, the last Wednesday and Thursday of July, for both commercial and non-commercial harvesters. Boaters and divers flock to the Keys for the annual event, which allows six spiny lobsters to be caught per person each day.

Tropical Fish

Florida is North America's primary exporter of tropical fish. There are over 200 fish farms in the state producing over 800 varieties of tropical fish. The industry dates back to the 1930s, when fish would be sent north via rail in steel milk crates. Air shipments made things much easier, and now, tropical fish are the second largest airfreight item (after citrus fruit) out of Florida's main airports. Over one million crates of live fish fly out of Florida each year.

Walking Catfish

You could say they're a fish out of water! Not only is the species now common in a state far, far away from their native Southeast Asia, these fish are also quite often literally out of the water. Nicknamed "Frankenfish" by the stunned residents who first encountered them, walking catfish (*Clarias batrachus*) are undoubtedly the strangest of the 34 current exotic species of fish that have found new homes in Florida. About 12 inches or so in length and sporting scaleless, mucus-covered skin, walking catfish can not only breathe air, but also use their pectoral fins to crawl overland from one body of water to another.

Nobody is quite sure how walking catfish arrived in the state, but as it is unlikely that they either swam or walked to Florida, walking catfish were probably introduced to Florida in the 1960s through the exotic fish trade. When they first appeared, there was great concern that they would wreak eco-havoc with other fish species. However, after an initial population boom, a balance seems to have been struck, and their numbers have declined over the past two decades.

Ironically, though not notably detrimental in nature, walking catfish have stepped all over the business that accidentally introduced them in the first place: aquaculture. They now frequently raid the ponds of fish farmers and eat all their "crops." As a result, fish farmers have been forced to build levees and fences to keep the marauders out.

SIX-TOED CATS

Sailors consider polydactyl cats good luck. Regular cats have five front toes and four back toes; polydactyls have six, sometimes even seven toes, and the extra claw helps give them supremely sturdy sea legs and unparalleled prowess when it came to hunting shipboard rodents. They were, and still are, considered a rarity—an extra digit isn't exactly the sort of quirk most cat breeders go for, and sailors themselves are generally too nomadic to be bothered.

One of the few places on Earth that a polydactyl colony has prospered is on Key West, an island sufficiently isolated to enable the genetic quirk to pass down over the years. The cats took root on the island when local author Ernest Hemingway was given one as a gift by a sea captain. After Hemingway's death in 1961, his former Key West home was turned into a museum, and its caretakers include taking care of his cats as part of the job description. There are now approximately 60 cats roaming the literary lion's old home, half of which sport extra digits. They are now nearly as big a draw for the museum as the author himself. Polydactyls are now popularly known as "Hemingway cats."

Not only is Miami's Metrozoo a cageless zoo, but it's the nation's only zoo located in a subtropical climate. Hurricane Andrew dealt the zoo a devastating blow on August 24, 1992. More than 5000 trees were lost, and Wings of Asia, the 1.5-acre, free-flight area was destroyed, along with 300 exotic Asian birds. Fortunately, the zoo reopened on December 18, 1992, and by July 1993, most of the animals and trees had been returned and reestablished. As of 2006, Metrozoo's 740 acres offer 81 exhibits and 1306 specimens.

GROUND SWELL

Size Matters

Even the most geographically challenged have little trouble pin-pointing Florida on a map. As you've probably noticed, Florida dangles all by itself off the country's underbelly, bearing more than a passing cartographical resemblance to a certain portion of the male anatomy!

According to the U.S. Census Bureau, Florida ranks 22nd among the states in size, with a total of 58,560 square miles. And if you decide to drive from Pensacola to Key West, you'll cover 792 miles of highway. Here are a few more details:

- ☛ Total land area: 54,136 square miles

- ☛ Total water area: 4424 square miles

- ☛ Length north to south (St. Mary's River to Key West): 447 miles

- ☛ Width east to west (Atlantic Ocean to Perdido River): 361 miles

- ☛ Geographic center: 12 miles northwest of Brooksville, Hernando County

- ☛ Coastline: 1197 miles

- ☛ Tidal shoreline: 2276 miles

- ☛ Beaches: 663 miles

Highest Points
The greatest elevation in Florida is found in the northern Panhandle not far from the Alabama border. Soaring a majestic 345 feet above sea level, the rarely snow-capped Britton Hill is part of the Florida Ridge Hills, and its paved summit is easily accessible via Road 285 in Walton County. Named for

a postmistress from the nearby town of Lakewood, Britton Hill is the lowest state high point in the entire country; it's a good 103 feet shorter than the closest runner-up, Delaware's Ebright Azimuth.

The highest point in peninsular Florida, meanwhile, is Sugarloaf Mountain, part of a gated golf community located outside Orlando. At just 312 feet above sea level, the members-only mountain is a mere molehill, especially compared to other Sugarloaf Mountains around the world such as the ones found in Oregon (7938 feet), California (6924 feet), Maine (4200 feet), Australia (3773 feet), Massachusetts (2030 feet), Wales (1955 feet), Ireland (1886 feet), Brazil (1296 feet), Maryland (1282 feet), Canada (1000 feet) and even modest Minnesota (500 feet).

FABULOUS FLORIDA

Peninsular Florida actually has another mountain that is a good seven feet taller than Sugarloaf, but it can't really be included because it is human-made. The Forbidden Mountain of Disneyworld's Expedition Everest roller coaster is the tallest of all the artificial Disney rides and peaks that include Big Thunder

Mountain, Space Mountain, Splash Mountain and Mount Gushmore. The Forbidden Mountain roller coaster is famous for going backwards as well as forwards, a change in direction caused by an animatronic abominable snowman forcing riders' retreat.

Deepest Point

Located in the Panhandle near Tallahassee, Wakulla Springs is the largest and deepest freshwater cave system in the world. The limestone caves were created when Florida rose from the sea for the last time 10 million years ago. More than 250 million gallons of water a day, or 40 thousand per minute, flow from the springs, forming a nine-mile-long underground river that stretches to the Gulf of Mexico. Nobody is quite sure just how deep this river truly is. So far, divers have descended over 300 feet into the caves, but the cavern forks into four channels tunneling deeply in different directions.

Wakulla Springs first piqued the interest of scientists back in 1850, when a local woman reported seeing what looked like mastodon bones down in the depths. It turns out she was right; since then, the remains of at least nine other extinct Ice Age creatures—including those of a saber-toothed tiger, giant sloth and American lion—have been discovered by divers in the spring's caves. Evidence has also been found of Paleo-Indian inhabitants from over 12,000 years ago.

DID YOU KNOW?

In the 1954 horror classic, *Creature from the Black Lagoon*, the lagoon in question—from which a monstrous fish-man emerged from to kidnap actress Julia Adams—was supposed to lie along the Amazon River. However, the body of water shown was actually located near Wakulla Springs. The spring's crystal-clear waters were ideal for filming the early black-and-white film's underwater sequences.

Longest River

The 310-mile-long St. Johns River is the longest river in Florida and one of the longest northward-flowing rivers in the country. Commonly misspelled as the St. John's, the river basin was originally home to the Timucua people, who called the slow-moving waterway *Welaka*, or "River of Lakes." Sarcastic Spanish explorers gave it the unlikely name *Río de Corrientes*, or "River of Currents," while more prosaic French Huguenots, who landed at its mouth in May 1562, gave it the name *Rivière du Mai*, or "River of May." The elevation change from the river's headwaters to its mouth is only about 30 feet, making the St. Johns one of the world's laziest rivers. The river begins in the marshes near Cape Canaveral and eventually empties into the ocean near Jacksonville.

The city of Jacksonville has always had a strong connection to the St. Johns River. In fact, the city was originally known as "Cowford" because it was located where the river was narrow and shallow enough for cattle to wade across. Although the river is now highly polluted, it's not uncommon to see dolphins and manatees in it to the east of Jacksonville.

 Florida is the only state that has two different rivers with the same name. There is a Withlacoochee River in north-central Florida and another Withlacoochee River in central Florida. The name comes from a Seminole phrase meaning "crooked river."

Largest Lake

Florida's largest lake is the fourth largest lake located wholly within American borders after Lake Michigan, Alaska's Lake Iliamna and Utah's Great Salt Lake. Covering over 700 square miles, but less than 10 feet deep, Lake Okeechobee gets its name from the Seminole words *oki* (water) and *chubi* (big), and so literally means "big water." Known locally as Lake O, the Big O or simply the Lake, it was formed about 6000 years ago when glacier waters receded from the mainland. Today, it serves as the spigot for the vast swamps of the Everglades. As big as the lake is, you can't actually see it from the road. Okeechobee is barely above sea level.

The lake burst its banks when a hurricane blew through in 1928, killing thousands of people. As a result, it's now surrounded by the 140-mile-long, three-story Hoover Dike, which is part of the Florida National Scenic Trail, a 1400-mile footpath from Big Cypress National Preserve (located between Miami and Naples) to the Panhandle. A system of canals provides outlets to the Atlantic Ocean and the Gulf of Mexico. The lake is literally the lifeblood of southern Florida, providing drinking water for millions of people and supporting the state's $1.5 billion agriculture industry. It is also a world-class sport-fishing and birdwatching destination.

DID YOU KNOW?

Comprising a wide diversity of habitats, Florida has three million acres of lakes, ponds and reservoirs, ranking third among all 50 states in water area, after Alaska and Michigan. It's also home to Lake DeFuniak, one of only two perfectly round natural lakes. The spring-fed lake is about one mile in circumference and was probably caused by a meteor crashing into the Panhandle untold centuries ago.

On the Beaches

Life truly is a beach in Florida, a state that's essentially an enormous, overdeveloped sandspit. Three-quarters of its 1197-mile-long coastline is made of sandy beaches, and not a single spot within Florida is more than 60 miles from any one of them. Beaches are the number one recreational destination for Americans, and the Sunshine State's can be broken down into three different types:

☛ The Atlantic Coast: the sand is generally darker and coarser than elsewhere in Florida. Beaches, particularly along the northeast coast, are often packed hard enough to drive cars on (Daytona Beach, for example, is practically a coastal highway). Because the coast is unprotected, the waves that roll in are large and good for surfing.

☛ The Gulf Coast: the sand is softer and whiter, the water clearer, and—apart from when hurricanes are passing through—the waves smaller.

☛ The Panhandle: sand dunes abound, and the more remote beaches are much less busy.

Son of a Beach

Since 1991, Florida International University professor Stephen "Doctor Beach" Leatherman has been releasing annual rankings of America's top 10 beaches. After carefully considering criteria ranging from sand softness and water temperature to riptides and scenery, his 2006 list put Caladesi Island State Park, near the town of Dunedin, in the number two national spot, while Barefoot Beach Park in Bonita Springs finished in 10th place. It's worth noting that past number one winners—including Bahia Honda State Park in the Florida Keys, St. Andrews State Park in Panama City, Fort DeSoto Park in St. Petersburg, St. Joseph Peninsula State Park in Port St. Joe and Grayton Beach State Park in Santa Rosa—are all automatically excluded from the most recent rankings.

Due South

Every day, hundreds of tourists pose for photos beside a large cement buoy in Key West that mistakenly marks the southern-most point of the continental United States. Being an island, Key West isn't part of the continental U.S. at all, and in any case, it isn't even the southernmost part of Florida; that claim to fame belongs to Ballast Key, a private island southwest of Key West. In fact, the marker isn't even the southernmost part of Key West; that honor belongs to a spot lying hidden behind the barbed wire of a U.S. Navy base. The actual southernmost point in continental America is located in Everglades National Park, which, for the record, is still well north of Hawaii.

EXPLORING FLORIDA'S NATIONAL PARKS

Biscayne National Park

There aren't many hiking trails in Biscayne National Park, as the vast majority of it is made of water. Located within sight of downtown Miami, the park preserves Biscayne Bay, one of the top scuba diving and snorkeling destinations in America. Glass-bottomed boat tours and canoes or kayaks are also popular ways to explore Biscayne's aquamarine waters and deserted islands.

The 207-square-mile park is part of the world's third largest reef, after Australia's Great Barrier Reef and offshore Belize. Despite looking like a big chunk of rock, the reef is a living, breathing organism composed of millions of tiny coral polyps that extract calcium from the seawater and grow one to 16 feet every millennium.

 Biscayne's Maritime Heritage Trail is the only underwater archaeological trail in the National Park system. The Shipwreck Trail includes six wrecks spanning a century of maritime history. One of the most interesting is the wreck of the steamer *Alicia*, which ran aground in 1905 bound from Spain to Cuba. It was laden with cargo valued at greater than $1 million, including fine silk, silverware, pianos, cases of fine alcohol and even a fully complete iron bridge. The ensuing, often violent battles between dozens of different groups of looters resulted in the creation of new American salvage laws.

Dry Tortugas National Park

Accessible only via boat or seaplane, Dry Tortugas National Park is located about 70 miles west of Key West in the Gulf of

Mexico. The tiny archipelago of seven islands within the 101-square-mile park was first named by explorer Juan Ponce de León, who named them *Las Tortugas* (The Turtles) because of the many different types of sea turtles residing there. The "dry" was later added by sailors as a warning that there was no fresh-water to be found. One of the park's larger islands, Bush Key, has been designated a wildlife sanctuary to protect the nesting grounds of the sooty tern. The bird's annual nesting season between February and September draws an estimated 100,000 terns and boatloads of binocular-toting birdwatchers.

Everglades National Park

The Everglades are generally considered a national treasure. Designated a World Heritage Site and an International Biosphere Reserve, it is the most famous wetland on Earth and the largest subtropical wilderness in the continental United States. Less than a century ago, however, it was thought of as merely a mosquito-infested wasteland that needed to be somehow drained, settled and put to productive use. By doing so, one of the country's greatest natural wonders became an ecological disaster zone.

The entire region known as the Everglades, of which the actual national park makes up only about 20 percent, is sometimes known as the River of Grass. Although it appears flatter than a pancake, the limestone shelf that the Everglades perch on actually has a slight southward tilt that gives the swamp water a direction in which to flow. Extending from Lake Okeechobee down to Florida Bay and the Gulf of Mexico, the Everglades encompass 2100 square miles and contain both the largest mangrove forest and the slowest-moving river in the world. Essentially a shallow, slow-moving flood inches deep and miles wide, the name "Everglades" comes from a corruption of the name "River Glades." The nickname was bestowed on the swamp by an 18th-century British surveyor because of the area's abundant saw grass, a hostile plant with sharp, jagged edges that grows as high as 12 feet. The northern part of the Everglades consists of a prairie covered by shallow water, while the southern regions are mostly made up of salt marshes and mangrove swamps.

Swamp Stomped

In 1845, the year Florida joined the Union, fewer than 100 white people resided in South Florida. But by the end of the 19th century, more than seven million people lived there, and millions more visited annually. And they needed water. In 1906, the Army Corps of Engineers first began the enormous task of draining and rechannelling the circulatory system of the Everglades in an attempt to make the land suitable for farming and to provide drinking water for the swelling population. Their mission was accomplished, but there was a high price to be paid: over half of the original Everglades are now sprawling suburbs and sugar plantations.

Although the southern Everglades below the Tamiami Trail were preserved in 1947 as a national park, this area soon deteriorated into an ecological mess. The River of Grass stopped flowing, former wetlands began catching fire and 90 percent of its resident birds vanished.

DID YOU  KNOW?

In 2000, Republicans and Democrats finally found something to agree on and dedicated almost $8 billion to the Comprehensive Everglades Restoration Plan, the largest ecosystem restoration project in America's history. The government has bought land around Lake Okeechobee in the hope of creating new marshes that will store water and filter out toxic chemicals before releasing the additional water into the wetlands to the south. Meanwhile, the Army Corps of Engineers has begun plans to reconnect the various parts of the Everglades that have suffered from the building of artificial barriers and drainage canals.

OTHER NATIONAL WILDERNESS AREAS

Apalachicola National Forest

Located along the east bank of the Apalachicola River, this is the largest U.S. National Forest in Florida and the only one found in the Panhandle. Apalachicola was the setting for a memorable episode of the television series *The X-Files*; in that episode, mutated survivors of Ponce de León's expedition to find the Fountain of Youth were roaming the present-day forest and preying on unwary hunters.

Big Cypress National Preserve

There aren't actually many big cypress trees left in Big Cypress; most were chopped down for lumber before the preserve was created. Actually, the name was given to reflect the preserve's considerable size of more than 720,000 acres (1125 square miles). Located near Lake Okeechobee, Big Cypress plays a crucial role in the Everglades ecosystem, as rains that flood the preserve's "prairies" and wetlands eventually filter down through the Glades. Big Cypress, along with Big Thicket National Preserve in Texas, became the first of America's national preserves when both were established on October 11, 1974.

Canaveral National Seashore (CANA)

Home to more than 1000 plant species and 310 bird species, Canaveral's 24-mile-long beach is the longest undeveloped beach on Florida's east coast. Occupying 58,000 acres (90 square miles), CANA was established by an Act of Congress on January 3, 1975. Access to the park is occasionally restricted because of the activities of the barrier island's most famous tenant, the John F. Kennedy Space Center.

Choctawhatchee National Forest

Visitors are no longer welcome in Florida's fourth national forest. President Theodore Roosevelt first set aside the Panhandle forest for preservation on November 27, 1908, but Congress transferred 340,890 acres (more than 532 square miles) of the Choctawhatchee from the Forest Service to the War Department to use for training purposes in 1940. Choctawhatchee now hosts Eglin Air Force Base, one of the largest air force bases in the world, employing more than 8500 military personnel and around 4500 civilians.

Gulf Islands National Seashore

Spanning 150 miles from Mississippi to Florida, the barrier islands of America's largest national seashore contain countless beaches, bayous and crumbling military forts. It is also a popular place for sea turtles—four of a total of seven species nest on Gulf Islands National Seashore. Florida's portion of the seashore also contains the Naval Live Oaks Reservation, located near Gulf Breeze. Covering more than 1300 acres (two square miles), this stand of oak trees was first planted by the U.S. Navy in 1828 because, back then, oak was highly prized for shipbuilding. Unfortunately, recent hurricanes have since flattened many of these beautiful trees.

Ocala National Forest

Established in 1908, Ocala is the oldest national forest east of the Mississippi River, the southernmost national forest in the continental U.S. and the most visited in Florida. Ocala is also the state's second largest national forest, covering about 607 square miles. Housing one of Central Florida's last remaining traces of forested land, the area has the largest concentration of sand pine in the world, as well as some of the best remaining stands of longleaf pine in the state. A portion of Ocala known as the Pinecastle Bombing Range, the only place on the east coast where the Navy can do live impact training, sees an average of 20,000 bombs—some live—dropped on it each year.

Osceola National Forest

Covering 200,000 acres (more than 312 square miles), Osceola National Forest has almost completely regrown since the early part of the 20th century, when its pine flatwoods were mostly wiped out by heavy timbering. Named in honor of the Seminole warrior Osceola, the national forest was created by President Herbert Hoover in 1931. Located about 50 miles west of Jacksonville, the forest was also the site of Florida's largest Civil War battle, one that the Confederates won.

That Sinking Feeling...

Florida, especially the northern region, holds the dubious distinction of being the number one state for sinkholes. Also known as sinks, shake holes, swallow holes or swallets, these geological oddities occur when part of the underground aquifer erodes and/or large voids develop. Normally, these voids fill with water and support the ground above. But when the surface becomes saturated (and Florida is no stranger to wetness), the voids may weaken and collapse, leaving noticeable and destructive holes in the ground. And although most sinkholes aren't usually small, they can really grow. One sinkhole that formed near Winter Park in 1981 expanded to 320 feet wide and 90 feet deep in a single day! This mighty hole went on to swallow a public pool, a car dealership and a huge area of a major city street.

In Gainesville, sinkholes even attract tourists. The city boasts Devil's Millhopper Geological State Park, which features a sinkhole measuring more than 492 feet wide and 118 feet deep. The park has 232 winding steps that take visitors to the bottom.

COME ONE, COME ALL

Top 10 Attractions

Having a chapter dedicated to Florida's major tourist attractions is a bit redundant when the words "Florida" and "tourism" are practically synonymous. Tourism is the Sunshine State's biggest industry, with an estimated annual economic impact of nearly $60 billion. Pretty much everyone has already heard all about its major draws, such as the golf courses and beaches, Busch Gardens, the Kennedy Space Center, Epcot Center and, of course, Disneyworld. Here is a top 10 list of some of Florida's less crowded and more offbeat attractions.

America's First Dead White Guy Memorial

Who the expired Spaniard actually was remains a mystery, but discounting the discovery of buried Viking bones, he evidently was the first white man to draw his final breath on what is now American soil. The memorial is located next to the town of Punta Gorda's main boat ramp in Ponce de León Park. A plaque now commemorates his death by arrows fired by the Caloosa tribe in 1513.

Coral Castle

Nobody is quite sure how someone only 5 feet tall and weighing around 100 pounds managed to single-handedly build a towering castle out of two million pounds of coral rock. What *is* known is that Homestead resident Edward Leedskalnin, a lovesick Latvian immigrant, spent 28 years building the vast structure, mostly at night when no one was watching, in a spectacularly unsuccessful attempt to win back the heart of Agnes Scuffs, who'd dumped him on the day before their wedding. The castle at the intersection of South Dixie Highway and Biscayne Drive contains not only coral walls but also coral chairs, a bed and heart-shaped table, and the castle's true *pièce*

de résistance, a massive coral gate that could be opened with the push of a button. Leedskalnin died in 1951, and the castle opened as a tourist attraction two years later. Unlike other South Florida structures built to code, it has survived countless storms without a scratch. Sadly, Agnes never came to see the castle built in her honor.

The Psychic Capital of the World

Cassadaga, a tiny village located on the outskirts of Deltona, was founded in 1895 by George P. Colby, a New York spiritualist who experienced a vision telling him he needed to travel south and establish a new spiritualist community somewhere warmer. Now home to a busy community of mediums, clairvoyants, healers, palm-readers, and other like-minded sorts, Cassadaga bills itself as the oldest active religious community in the southeastern United States and was added to the National Register of Historic Places in 1991. One of the town's more infamous attractions is known as the Devil's Chair, a bench in the local graveyard. Rumor has it that if you sit on the bench at midnight, the Devil will appear. But if you'd rather not meet the Devil, you can offer him a beer—legend has it that if you leave an unopened can or bottle on the chair overnight, it will be empty by morning yet still be unopened.

Captain Tony's Saloon

Located at 428 Green Street in Key West, Captain Tony's is the oldest licensed saloon in the state. Captain Tony's was known as Sloppy Joe's back in the days when it was Ernest Hemingway's favorite drinking hole (he immortalized the establishment as Freddy's Bar in the novel *To Have and Have Not*) during his decade living in Key West. Other luminaries, such as Tennessee Williams, Robert Frost, Elizabeth Taylor, Jimmy Buffet (who gave the place further fame with his song "Last Mango in Paris") and presidents Harry Truman and John F. Kennedy have also all stopped by for a drink or two over the years. The current proprietary publican, Tony Tarracino, is something of a legend in his own right. A former charter boat captain, gun runner for Cuban revolutionaries (the forgettable film *Cuba Crossing,* based on his experiences and starring Stuart Whitman, came out in 1980), and mayor of Key West, Captain Tony, is currently the island's official Goodwill Ambassador.

Burt Reynolds and Friends Museum

Mustachioed movie star Burt Reynolds was the first person to make a million bucks a movie, and the Palm Beach town of Jupiter is awfully proud of its most famous part-time resident. Open only from 10:00 AM to 4:00 PM, Friday through Sunday, at 100 North Highway 1, this vast collection of Burt-related memorabilia includes such important artifacts as his canoe from *Deliverance,* his hotrod from *Smokey and the Bandit,* his football helmet from *The Longest Yard,* his hat from *100 Rifles,* and his Vaseline-lined cowboy boots from *Striptease.* Gifts from Burt's buddies on display include a pair of Muhammad Ali's boxing gloves, one of Roy Rogers' old saddles, letters from Frank Sinatra and Carol Burnett, and autographed jerseys from Bobby Orr, Dan Marino and Joe Montana.

The World's Largest Alligator

At just over 200 feet long, "Swampy" is the largest alligator ever. Fortunately, Swampy is artificial and doesn't require feeding. The gigantic gator houses the gift shop, ticket counter and offices of Jungle Adventures, a theme park/gator farm in the town of Christmas, which is halfway between Orlando and Titusville. The park specializes in exotic animals and mock Native American villages. Swampy is a good 74 feet longer than the world's second largest alligator, which can be found at Jungle Land, a theme park/gator farm in the town of Kissimmee that specializes in exotic animals and mock 16th-century Spanish forts.

Drive-in Church

Car culture and Christianity collide in a converted drive-in movie theater located at 3140 South Atlantic Avenue in Daytona Beach. Every Sunday since 1953, members of the Disciples of Christ Church and anyone else curious have been gathering in this unique parking lot of worship featuring sermons and sing-alongs, where the faithful honk their horns instead of clapping.

Edison and Ford Winter Estates

Two of America's most famous inventors spent their winters in Florida and were next door neighbors. The Edison and Ford Winter Estates, located at 2350 McGregor Boulevard in Fort Myers, preserves the properties of both Thomas Edison and Henry Ford. The grounds along the bank of the Caloosahatchee River include the laboratory where Edison first created the phonograph, and a vast botanical garden featuring plants from around the world, including a 400-foot banyan tree, the largest tree in Florida.

The World's Only Underwater Hotel

Jules' Undersea Lodge is named after Jules Verne, the author of *20,000 Leagues Under the Sea*, but is itself only submerged 30 feet. A former underwater research center located in Emerald Lagoon off Key Largo, the 600-square-foot building features two separate bedrooms, hot showers, a kitchen and all the comforts of home, as well as 42-inch windows to watch the lagoon's passing wildlife. Although most guests are scuba enthusiasts, hotel staff can assist those who've never gone diving before in getting inside.

Salvador Dali Museum

Even though the master surrealist artist never actually visited the Sunshine State himself, Florida is nonetheless the home of the world's most comprehensive collection of the renowned Spanish artist's works. Located at 1000 Third Street South in the city of St. Petersburg, the museum includes seven of his 18 giant masterpiece paintings, including *Galacidalacidesoxiribunucleicacid*, *The Hallucinogenic Toreador* and *The Discovery of America by Christopher Columbus*. There are also 95 oil paintings, over 100 watercolors and drawings, and 1300 graphics, photographs, sculptures and other objets d'art.

OH, THE HUMANITY

Population Information

According to the American Census Bureau, three states—Florida, California and Texas—will account for nearly one-half (46 percent) of the country's total population growth between 2000 and 2030. Consequently, Florida, now the fourth most populous state behind California, Texas and New York, will squeeze past New York for third place in total population by 2011.

As of 2006, Florida's population stands at 18,089,888, an increase of over 13 percent from 2000. The state now ranks as the eighth most crowded, with 296.4 people per square mile (New Jersey, the most crowded, has 1134.4 people per square mile), and the ninth fastest growing, with a 1.8 percent increase in population in 2006 (Arizona grew by 3.6 percent).

In terms of new arrivals, Florida is the second fastest growing state behind only Texas; research suggests that as many as 1000 people move to Florida each day. The state's center of population is located in the town of Lake Wales in Polk County.

DID YOU  KNOW?

Florida may be a melting pot, attracting visitors and residents from all corners of the globe, but the two largest groups living in the state are Yankees, defined as hailing from the Northeast and Midwest, and Crackers, defined as those born in Georgia or Florida.

Ten Largest Cities in Florida

City	Population
Jacksonville	782,623
Miami	386,614
Tampa	325,989
St. Petersburg	249,079
Hialeah	220,485
Orlando	213,223
Fort Lauderdale	170,824
Tallahassee	158,500
Pembroke Pines	150,685
Hollywood	138,412

DID YOU KNOW?

About 95 percent of all Floridians live in the state's 19 metropolitan areas.

Old Folks At Home

At the turn of the millennium, not one of the country's 50 states—not even Florida—had more people aged 65 or older than they did under 18. Today, over 23 percent of Florida's population is 65 years or older. Research shows that by 2030, more than one in every four residents in six states—Florida, Wyoming, Maine, New Mexico, Montana and North Dakota—will be 65 or older.

FABULOUS FLORIDA Counties in Florida with the largest percentage of senior citizens are Charlotte (35 percent), Citrus (32 percent), Highlands (33 percent), Hernando (31 percent) and Sarasota (32 percent).

The Foreign Component

More than half of Miami-Dade County's residents were born in another country, the highest rate of any American county. These foreign-born residents make up 51.4 percent of the county's population of 2.3 million. Neighboring Broward County ranks second among Florida's counties and 17th nationally, with 27.7 percent of the population hailing from other countries. Hialeah is the nation's number one city for Spanish speakers, with about 92 percent of the population speaking Spanish as their first language.

Among all U.S. cities, Tarpon Springs is home to the largest percentage of Greek Americans. In the early 1900s, Greek sponge divers settled in Tarpon Springs and developed the world's largest sponge industry.

Religious Differences

The majority of Floridians are Christian, and the majority of Christians are Protestant, although the Roman Catholic population is growing as a result of immigration. Florida, especially the southern part, is home to the largest Jewish community among all Southern states.

Religion	Percentage
Christian	82 percent
Protestant	54 percent
Roman Catholic	26 percent
Baptist	19 percent
Other Protestant	16 percent
Methodist	6 percent
Jewish	4 percent
Presbyterian	4 percent
Episcopal	3 percent
Lutheran	3 percent
Pentecostal	3 percent
Other Christian	2 percent
Other Religions	1 percent
Non-Religious	13 percent

The Name Game

Attention all Florida-based, soon-to-be mommies and daddies! Have you been fruitlessly searching for just the right moniker for your little prince or princess? Well, the Social Security Administration has revealed the most frequently given baby names and their number of occurrences for the Sunshine State, circa 2005:

Boys			Girls		
1.	Joshua	1489	1.	Emily	1292
2.	Michael	1476	2.	Isabella	1269
3.	Anthony	1318	3.	Madison	1091
4.	Christopher	1296	4.	Emma	877
5.	Jacob	1249	5.	Sophia	826
6.	Daniel	1239	6.	Ashley	792
7.	Matthew	1224	7.	Samantha	745
8.	Alexander	1102	8.	Brianna	734
9.	Nicholas	1094	9.	Hannah	717
10.	David	1060	10.	Olivia	696

IT'S JUST A LITTLE BIT OF HISTORY

Dino No-No...
At times, the behavior of Floridians may seem a little prehistoric. But evidence shows that actual dinosaurs never roamed the Florida landscape. You see, the land that now makes up the Sunshine State was entirely underwater at the time. However, a huge array of fish, bird and mammal fossils has been unearthed within the state's borders. These include a giant beaver and giant armadillo, and also a mastodon skeleton, which is on display in the Museum of Florida History.

The Truth About the Youth Sleuth

In 1513, Juan Ponce de León first set foot on the North American continent, most likely near present-day St. Augustine. Loyal to Spain, León was on an epic quest for the mythical Fountain of Youth. And while he may not have actually discovered the Fountain of Youth, he did succeed in discovering—and naming—the state, in the name of Spain. León was eventually killed by an Indian-fired poison arrow in 1521. Oh, and the fountain? If it even exists, possible Florida locations include Silver Springs, Green Cove Springs, the St. Johns River, Miami's Bal Harbor and Sarasota.

Long Live St. Augustine

St. Augustine is the oldest continuously inhabited city in the U.S. The record-holder for the first Florida (and national) establishment is held by Fort Caroline, founded in 1564 by French Huguenots and destroyed by their mortal enemies, the Spanish, just one year later!

Battle Prowess, Yes! Financial Prowess, No!

The Spanish may have excelled as conquerors, but their business sense leaves much to be desired. To obtain Florida, the U.S. government agreed to pay American and Spanish civilians up to $5 million in war damage, while also dropping claim to Texas, in what was known as the Onis-Adams Treaty. However, America never got around to paying their bill to the Spanish. When all was said and done, the U.S. only shelled out about $200,000 in actual damage claims!

An Offer They Can Refuse

Back in the 1700s, Florida was divided into two colonies: East Florida, under the flag of Spain, and West Florida, under the flag of Britain. At the conclusion of the Seven Years' War, Spain was forced to hand over all territories east of the Mississippi River to Britain under the terms of the 1763 Treaty of Paris. During the Revolutionary War, Floridians were loyal to the British. In fact, they actually passed on the chance to be one of the original 13 colonies! These residents depended on the British for protection against attacks from the Natives. The territory soon became a haven for British-loyal Americans, and the area prospered.

Southern Pride

Even though Florida was considered militarily insignificant, there was some action to be seen on its soil. On February 20, 1864, 10,000 soldiers met in the Battle of Olustee. Also referred to as the Battle of Ocean Pond, it was the largest Civil War battle fought in the state. The Union's 5500 soldiers marched into Florida to sever Confederate supply routes, secure Union enclaves and recruit black soldiers. But the mission ran into some difficulties—in the form of 5000 Confederate soldiers—near the town of Olustee.

The battle raged, and eventually, the Union was forced to retreat. When all was said and done, 203 Union soldiers had been killed, 1152 were wounded and 506 were missing. On the Confederate side, 93 were killed, 847 were wounded and six were missing. The Union's embarrassing defeat led Northern lawmakers to do some serious thinking—namely, why the North even needed to bother with Florida in the first place! Today, this battlefield is part of Olustee Battlefield Historic State Park, which boasts an annual historical reenactment and festival.

DID YOU KNOW?

Smack dab in the middle of nowhere might not be the place you'd expect to find the largest 19th-century American coastal fortress. Construction on Fort Jefferson, the largest masonry structure in the Western Hemisphere, began in 1846 to protect U.S. interests in the Gulf. However, the fort was abandoned, still unfinished, 30 years and 16 million bricks later, after the double-whammy of a hurricane and a deadly outbreak of yellow fever. The fort was used as a prison during the Civil War for Union deserters, as well as for others, including the infamous Dr. Samuel Mudd, who were jailed for their involvement in the assassination of Abraham Lincoln.

FABULOUS FLORIDA

Fort Zachary Taylor in Key West admirably served as a Union stronghold. Union forces led by Captain John Brannon used this site to successfully block Confederate ships. It's thought that his actions shortened the length of the Civil War by as much as a full year. Later, Fort Zachary Taylor saw action in the Spanish-American War and both World Wars.

Miami's Number One Citizen: Julia Tuttle

Miami is renowned the world over for its thriving nightlife, beautiful beaches and well-deserved reputation as a center of international big business. However, a little more than a century ago, this mighty metropolis was nothing more than a bug-filled, backwater swamp. The Miami of the new millennium came about because of the efforts of one woman, Julia Tuttle. Known as the "Founding Mother of Miami," Tuttle recognized the inherent possibilities of the area.

In December 1894, Florida was struck by a freak, 36-hour, killer cold snap. As a result, the entire citrus crop of the northern half of the state was wiped out. However, Southern Florida, and Miami specifically, was spared the freezing fate. And Tuttle, who had bought an enormous citrus plantation in 1891, now had the only available citrus in the whole state! She was able to convince railroad magnate Henry Flagler to expand his Florida East Coast Railroad to Miami. The city's potential was realized, and on July 28, 1896, Miami was officially incorporated as a city. Today, the Julia Tuttle Causeway connects Miami and Miami Beach.

The Saga of the Barefoot Mailmen

No doubt, you've heard the unofficial motto of the United States Postal Service: "Neither snow nor rain nor heat nor gloom of night stays these couriers from the swift completion of their appointed rounds." But in some parts of the country, quick and efficient postal delivery was easier said than done, especially when it came to the Southeast Florida of yesteryear. Truthfully, the entire state owes a great debt to those hearty pioneers known as the barefoot mailmen.

In the 1880s, the area was still a wild and undiscovered region, with few people and fewer roads. But times were changing, and more and more people were arriving, attracted by cheap land and the allure of citrus farming. And these new citizens required communication and contact in the form of quicker mail delivery. Previously, mail was delivered by boat, and it took anywhere from three months to a year for a letter to reach its final destination. Soon, a post office was built for the growing population, and the bustling mail route from Jupiter to Miami was split in two.

Hearty, physically fit men were needed for mail delivery. Because there wasn't enough water for horses and no trails along the shoreline, the work was done on foot—hence the nickname. The long trip was tempered by kind customers and existing shelters that provided a roof over the carriers' heads. But these men still faced grueling conditions—bad-to-horrible weather, unbearable heat and humidity, hostile wildlife, irritating insects and exhaustion. And they carried the mail, plus their water and all of their supplies, on their backs. But the mail had to be delivered!

James Edward Hamilton, a Kentucky native and citrus farmer, recognized a great opportunity and was awarded the contract for the southern portion of the route, from Hypoluxo to Miami. Hamilton was able to complete his round-trip route in a mere six days, a remarkable achievement! And he kept on succeeding until Monday, October 10, 1887, his final trip.

When Hamilton failed to return by Saturday, a search party was sent out. Eventually, they found his knapsack, mail pouch and personal belongings at Hillsboro Inlet, and it appeared that the boat he used was moved. Unfortunately, Hamilton himself was never found. Most people believed that he drowned in rough waters, but others thought he had been attacked by animals or local men.

The era of the barefoot mailmen came to an end in 1892, with the construction of a rock road between Jupiter and Miami. Nevertheless, these brave men—especially James Edward Hamilton—were instrumental in the history of Florida. Today, the lighthouse near the Hillsboro Inlet bears a plaque honoring Hamilton and his peers.

No Nukes is Good Nukes!

South Florida and Cuba have developed a close relationship—whether they wanted to or not! So it's a foregone conclusion that the Cuban Missile Crisis was bound to have an effect on Miami and the surrounding neighborhoods. For instance, surface to air missiles were not uncommon in the city limits at the time.

And then there's the matter of the corner of Kendall Drive and 127 Avenue. According to unsubstantiated reports, there may have been a storehouse for nuclear missiles at that location, following the events of the Missile Crisis. A barbed wire fence and a 10-foot-high, hill keep out pesky intruders and reporters (and not in that order)!

DID YOU KNOW?

Jacksonville has always prided itself on its naval heritage and the patriotism of its citizens. During the 1991 Gulf War, the city was home to the country's busiest military port. In fact, it shipped more supplies and people than any other port in the country.

ON THE MAP

The Panhandle

The Florida Panhandle is known as "the other Florida." Parts of the region have more of a Deep South feel, boast different trees and foliage and even exist in a different time zone. In fact, Pensacola, because of its location in the farthest reaches of northwestern Florida—it's actually as far west as Chicago—has been courted by Alabama to secede three times. But the ever-loyal city keeps turning down the offer.

Sunken Treasure

Why does Florida's Treasure Coast have that nickname? Well, there may be as much as $3 billion in treasure submerged off the coast! In 1715, a fleet of Spanish galleons hauling a fortune in possibly stolen silver, gold, diamonds and emeralds was hit by a hurricane off Florida's east coast, sending all 1000 sailors to a watery grave. In 1964, treasure hunter Mel Fisher unearthed the

ruins of one of the sunken ships, the *Nuestra Señora de las Nieves*, but found only $3 to $5 million worth of treasure. However, archaeologists had a field day as they uncovered such booty as belt buckles and the ship's wooden figurehead.

The Mouse's Mouth?

Boca Raton holds a worldwide reputation as an enclave of the rich and pampered. And that's why the city's name has always been a source of embarrassment, as it translates to "rat's mouth." But the truth is, the Spanish word *boca*, meaning "mouth," can be used to describe an inlet, while *raton*, meaning "mouse," was a term used by Spanish sailors to describe rocks that gnawed at a ship's cable.

 Key West was formerly known as *Cayo Hueso* (Bone Key) because the bones of Native Americans were found scattered along the shore.

Danish Dania

Most of Dania Beach's original 35 residents were of Danish ancestry, and they changed the name from "Modello" to "Dania." Broward County's first city, Dania, dates back to the 1880s and was incorporated in November 1904.

Sweet Miami

Miami is from the Tequesta word *mayaimi*, which is translated as "sweet water."

Water Everywhere

Hypoluxo is a Seminole expression meaning "water all around, no get out."

City Slogans and Nicknames

Anna Maria: Florida's Famous Year-Round Rest

Clearwater: Lightning Capital of the World

Clewiston: America's Sweetest Town

Coconut Creek: Butterfly Capital of the World

Crystal River: Where Man and Manatee Play

Daytona: Heart of Sunnyland; Big Beach, Big Fun

Eustis: City of Bright Tomorrows

Fort Myers: City of Palms; Gulf Coast Paradise

Gainesville: Hogtown; Where Nature and Culture Meet

Hallandale: Southernmost Canadian City

Hialeah: City of Progress

Jacksonville: Bold New City of the South; River City

Lake Worth: Where the Tropics Begin

Miami: Gateway to the Americas; The Magic City

Milton: A Perfect Place to Live and Work

Ocoee: Center of Good Living

Orlando: The City Beautiful; O-Town

Pensacola: City of Five Flags; Western Gate to the Sunshine State

St. Petersburg: The Sunshine City; Always in Season

Sebring: City of Health and Happiness; City of the Circle

Tallahassee: Capital City; All-Florida City

Tampa: Lightning Capital of the World; Big Guava

Venice: Shark Tooth Capital of the World

Wauchula: Cucumber Capital of the World

Winter Park: City of Culture and Heritage

Florida Cities' Claims to Fame

☛ In 1883, the St. James Hotel in Jacksonville became the first Florida building to have electricity.

☛ Eglin Air Force Base, near Valparaiso, is the home of the Western Hemisphere's largest military institution.

☛ DeFuniak Springs boasts one out of two of the world's only naturally round lakes.

☛ Ona is home to Solomon's Castle, a three-story structure made entirely from recycled materials.

☛ Plant City, also known as the "Winter Strawberry Capital of the World," earned a place in *Guinness World Records* for the world's largest strawberry shortcake. On February 19, 1999, an 827-square-foot, 6000-pound cake was baked in the city's McCall Park.

☛ Ochopee is the site of the smallest post office in the country.

☛ Carrabelle is famous for the world's smallest police station, which is housed in a telephone booth.

☛ Orlando attracts more visitors than any other American amusement park destination.

☛ Tampa's historic Ybor City district was renowned as the "Cigar Capital of the World." In its heyday, the city employed almost 12,000 *tabaqueros* (cigar-makers) in 200 factories, producing an estimated 700 million cigars every year.

☛ Until the 1850s, Key West was America's richest city per capita.

☛ Hailed as the "Shark Tooth Capital of the World," crowds have long been flocking to Venice to collect prehistoric sharks' teeth.

☛ Another Florida destination, Fort Lauderdale, is known as the "Venice of America" because of its 185 miles of local waterways.

☛ Down in the Florida Keys, Islamorada is regarded as the "Sports Fishing Capital of the World," while Key Largo has the nickname of "Dive Capital of the World."

And it should come as no surprise that Miami holds a few distinctions of its own:

☛ The world's largest banyan tree can be found in either Miami or India.

☛ Before the Florida East Coast Railroad expanded to Miami, the area was only accessible by boat.

☛ Greater Miami is unique among U.S. metropolitan areas in that it's bordered by two national parks: Everglades National Park and Biscayne National Park.

☛ The video game *Vice City* is modeled after Miami.

More Pressure Cooker than Melting Pot

According to a study released in January 2004, Miami holds a few unwanted records. In the "Sperling's Best Places" poll, which identified the most and least stressful U.S. cities, Miami was found to be the city with the highest violent crime rate and one of the highest property crime rates! Such factors as the city's high rates of unemployment and divorce, as well as long commuting times, contributed to the bad publicity. Take that, New York!

Malls Well that Ends Well!

Every year, millions of people flock to one of Florida's greatest resources: shopping malls. And the pinnacle of Sunshine State shopping is Sawgrass Mills in Sunrise. The mall boasts more than 500 stores on 2.5 million square feet of retail selling space, making it is the fourth largest mall in the United States, the largest in Florida and the largest outlet mall in the world!

CULINARY CONTRIBUTIONS

Restaurant Row

What with the rainbow of cultures choosing to call the Sunshine State home, it's no surprise that there is an endless buffet of culinary choices. And the population definitely takes advantage of this variety, as evidenced by a recent ZAGAT survey. It was found that South Floridians eat out more often than any other region in the country. The survey shows that Floridians eat out 3.8 times a week, compared to New York City's 3.4 times a week, Los Angeles' 3.7 times a week and Las Vegas' 3.6 times a week. *Mangia!*

Home of the Whopper

Miami is the birthplace—as well as the headquarters—of Burger King (BK). The worldwide fast food giant first opened for business on December 4, 1954, as "Insta Burger King." Ready to chow down on some more BK data?

☛ Burger King has restaurants in 61 countries.

☛ There are more than 11,220 BK outlets worldwide, though 66 percent are in the U.S.

☛ The company employs more than 340,000 people.

☛ Burger King welcomes an estimated 11.4 million customers daily.

Buffy Burgers

What's the connection between BK and *Buffy the Vampire Slayer*? Well, in 1982, four-year-old Sarah Michelle Gellar starred in a series of BK commercials, in which she declared that McDonald's burgers were 20 percent smaller than those of Burger King. This was the first time that a food chain went beyond the traditional vague rumors and actually named and attacked a competitor!

Where's Herb?

Another BK campaign—1985's $40 million "Where's Herb?" ads—made headlines as well. In the commercials, Herb was the only American man who had never eaten a Whopper, and any customers who spotted him won $5000. During Super Bowl XX, Burger King finally showed Herb to be a nerd with glasses and a bad suit. Herb was then sent on a multi-state media tour, including *The Today Show* and *Wrestlemania 2*. However, the campaign was a flop, and Herb was quickly dropped. In fact, *Advertising Age* magazine selected "Where's Herb?" as the "most elaborate advertising flop of the decade." Ouch!

Red Lobster

"For the seafood lover in you," we present…Florida's own Red Lobster! In 1968, the first location opened in Lakeland, where it was originally billed as a "harbor for seafood lovers." Today, the seafood favorite has locations in almost every state, as well as Canada and Japan. Both Red Lobster and another Florida-born chain, Olive Garden, are owned by the same parent company, Darden Restaurants. The former governor of Florida, Lawton "Walkin' Lawton" Chiles, was one of Red Lobster's initial investors.

Olive Garden

As the slogan says, "When you're here, you're family," and Olive Garden has succeeded in bringing the tastes and feel of Italy to hungry aficionados. Formed in Orlando in 1982, there are now almost 600 locations throughout the United States and Canada. In fact, research shows that Olive Garden is now the largest casual, full-service Italian restaurant chain in the world. The restaurant prides itself on its Italian appeal, even going so far as to model its newer locations after Tuscan-style farmhouses.

Outback Steakhouse

G'day mates! What's Tampa's Australian connection? Well, the city is the birthplace of none other than Outback Steakhouse, which opened in 1988. The restaurant chain's parent company also owns other popular theme restaurants around the country and the world, including Carraba's Italian Grill and St. Petersburg's Bonefish Grill.

Miami Subs Grill

In 1983, Greek immigrant Konstaninos "Gus" Boulis opened up a Key West sandwich shop called Mr. Submarine. Boulis—who later founded a popular line of casino cruises, known as SunCruz—did well, and the sub shop underwent a name change to Miami Subs Grill. In the 1990s, new shops opened throughout the state, and soon, nationwide. Miami Subs bought another chain, Arthur

Treacher's Fish and Chips, in 1998. Both chains were purchased by the Nathan's Famous hot dog chain in 1999, joining another Nathan's purchase, Kenny Rogers Roasters.

Boulis was ambushed and murdered on February 6, 2001, at the age of 51. The murder remained unsolved until September 2005, when police arrested three men: Anthony "Big Tony" Moscatiello, 67; Anthony "Little Tony" Ferrari, 48; and James "Pudgy" Fiorillo, 28. The murder may have had a connection to disgraced Washington, DC, lobbyist (and presidential friend) Jack Abramoff. In March 2006, Abramoff was sentenced to five years and 10 months in prison and ordered to pay $21 million in restitution for fraud, conspiracy and tax evasion. Just prior to his death, Boulis had sold a fleet of casino boats to Abramoff and his partner. However, both Abramoff and his partner denied any connection to Boulis' murder.

The Home of Hooters

Does the phrase "Delightfully Tacky, Yet Unrefined!" make you salivate? On October 4, 1983, a humble restaurant opened in Clearwater, content to offer hungry customers some tasty comfort food. Little did anyone predict that this establishment would launch an empire. The restaurant chain is Hooters, and today there are almost 450 locations in the United States and 20 other countries. The restaurant has spawned a merchandising juggernaut, and in the course of its history, it has employed more than 250,000 Hooters girls! But you only go there for the great food, right?

Women Only Need Apply

Need proof that lawyers will take on any case? In 1991, the Equal Employment Opportunities Commission (EEOC) brought forth a commissioner's charge against the Hooters chain. The charge? The agency claimed that Hooter's hiring practices discriminated against men. An exhaustive four-year investigation alerted the public to its startling findings: only women are hired as Hooters girls!

On November 15, 1995, the restaurant mobilized a march of 100 Hooters girls on Washington, DC. Legions of faithful Hooters fans, along with respected media outlets, gave their support, calling the EEOC's charge "another example of ridiculous government waste." This demonstration led Congress to request that the EEOC drop the matter. Later, additional class action suits challenged the chain's women-only hiring policies. But the resulting settlement decreed that only women would be hired as Hooters girls from that point on—a crushing blow for men who like to wear short shorts and a victory for people with eyesight!

Well, excuuuuse me! The name "Hooters" came from the wild and crazy guy, Steve Martin.

All Hail the Cookie King

Wallace Amos, better known as Famous Amos, was born in Tallahassee in 1936. The cookie connoisseur learned and perfected his sweet craft from his aunt, who taught him the importance of using just the right ingredients. In the case of his classic chocolate chip cookies, those ingredients included tasty treats not usually found in common cookie recipes, such as nutmeg. He joined the Air Force, but was honorably discharged—clearly, military service was not in the cards. In fact, during his time there, he was actually punished for misbehavior by having to work in the kitchen, and he used the occasion to make cookies.

In 1975, Amos took a friend's advice and opened his own cookie store, Famous Amos, in Los Angeles. He did all his own baking, which he based on his aunt's recipe, albeit with his special modifications (such as nutmeg). His new company began to expand across the U.S., and over 10 years, his company took off—he even began selling his cookies in Bloomingdale's! In 1985, mismanagement resulted in Amos selling off parts of his company, and in 1988, he was forced to sell to a larger corporation. He eventually started a new cookie company called Uncle Noname's Cookie Company. And that's the way the cookie crumbles!

Sloppy Joe's: More than a Watering Hole

Key West is home to one of the world's favorite destinations, a bar, restaurant and tourist attraction known as Sloppy Joe's. This landmark opened for business on December 5, 1933, the very day that Prohibition went down in flames. A former bootlegger, Joe Russell commemorated the occasion by opening the Blind Pig, a "legit" drinking establishment that soon became a favorite of noted Key West resident Ernest Hemingway. The author convinced Russell to change the bar's name to Sloppy Joe's, referring to the wet and messy floor.

On May 5, 1937, the entire bar moved across the street to its present location. Russell saved a ton on moving expenses, as the loyal customers picked up not only their drinks but also every item in the place and carried them to the new location. The new location featured the city's longest bar, a special gambling room and a 119-pound sailfish caught by Hemingway himself.

VICE SQUAD

No Champagne, No Gain

Planning on toasting with a miniature Champagne bottle? These small sizes, known as Balthazars, Methuselahs, Nebuchadnezzars or Salamanazars, may be the perfect complement to any occasion, but they're actually illegal in Florida!

Playing the Percentages

These are the statewide findings from the Centers for Disease Control and Prevention (CDC) for 2004. These percentages represent the total state population, unless otherwise noted.

Alcohol Consumption

Casual drinkers	56.3 percent
Heavy drinkers	5.3 percent

Alcohol-Related Traffic Fatalities

Total	1222
Per capita	0.687 per 10,000 people
As a percentage	38 percent (of all traffic fatalities)

Alcohol Abuse

Binge drinkers	12.4 percent
Alcohol abuse or dependence	7.09 percent
Needing treatment for alcohol use	6.84 percent

Here's to alcohol: the source of,
and answer to, all of life's problems.

–Homer Simpson

Tobacco Use

Everyday smokers	14.5 percent
Occasional smokers	5.6 percent
Total current smokers	20.1 percent
Former smokers	25.8 percent

Drug Use

Illicit drug use	8.7 percent
Cocaine use	2.52 percent
Marijuana use	10.57 percent

Florida's Drug Situation

The Sunshine State—likely because of the combination of its location, the quickly growing population and the incredible available cash flow—is a major player in the drug trade. As the endless number of news stories illustrates, Florida has become ground zero for international drug trafficking and money laundering organizations. And unfortunately, drug use is common around the state. Here's a rundown:

☞ Club drugs—Research suggests that ecstasy is the state's most readily available dangerous drug, and in fact, Florida ranks No. 1 in the U.S. for ecstasy seizures. Both LSD and GHB are also available, especially on college campuses.

☞ Cocaine—The primary drug of concern, cocaine is plentiful throughout the state. According to the National Drug Intelligence Center, Florida is the primary destination for cocaine smuggled from South America through the Caribbean and into the United States.

☞ Heroin—Between 1998 and 2001, Florida ranked second nationally for heroin seizures, with the central and southern regions recording the highest concentrations. Additionally,

Miami International Airport (MIA) has been found to be a major entry point for South American heroin into the country.

- Marijuana—There is a large amount of domestically grown and imported marijuana throughout the state. Studies show that the Panhandle is a leading transit area for the import of Mexican marijuana.

- Methamphetamine—Meth is the number one drug in Central Florida. There has also been an alarming increase in the number of meth lab seizures statewide. These labs produce an average of 1–2 ounces per batch.

Sex, Love and Marriage*

(*Not necessarily in that order)

Florida is no stranger to romance—and the end of it. Here are some revealing findings for 2004, according to the U.S. Census Bureau:

Households that are married-couple families	48.3 percent
Households that are married-couple families with their own children	17.9 percent
Households with one or more people under 18 years old	31.1 percent
Households with one or more people 65 years and over	29.6 percent
Married-couple families with both husband and wife in the labor force	46.1 percent
Divorce rate	about 4.5 per 1000 people
Men who never married	28.5 percent
Women who never married	22.5 percent

And here are some not-too-sexy sexual facts for the year 2005:

Teen birthrate per 1000 people	42.5
Abortion rate per 1000 people	26
Syphilis	Cases: 3282 Rate: 19.6 per 1000 people
Chlamydia	Cases: 42,382 Rate: 253.6 per 1000 people
Gonorrhea	Cases: 18,974 Rate: 113.5 per 1000 people
HIV testing rate	Ever tested: 57.2 percent Past 12 months: 32.4 percent
Annual reported HIV cases (all ages)	5107
Cumulative reported HIV cases	Adult/adolescent: 32,712 All ages: 33,048
Deaths from HIV	Total: 1719 Rate: 10.4 per 1000 people
New AIDS cases	All ages: 5822 Adult/adolescent: 5800 Pediatric: 22
AIDS case rate (all ages)	33.5 per 1000 people
Cumulative AIDS cases	Adult/adolescent: 95,208 All ages: 96,712 Per capita: 5.436 per 1000 people
Persons living with AIDS (all ages)	45,140
Deaths among persons with AIDS	53,244

Porcupine Lovin' and Other Weird Sexual Laws

☛ In Florida, it is actually against the law to commit any "unnatural acts" with another person. The good news? If you're caught corrupting the public morals, it is only a misdemeanor offense!

☛ Florida common law prohibits sexual intercourse unless performed in the missionary position.

☛ Unmarried couples are barred from committing "lewd acts."

☛ These unmarried couples are prohibited from living together in the same residence.

☛ One law makes it a crime to shower naked.

☛ If you kiss your wife's breasts, you are guilty of a crime.

☛ The laws of yesteryear make oral sex a crime, as well.

☛ And lastly, it's illegal (and painful) to have sexual relations with a porcupine!

Porn O' Plenty

One of the most profitable films ever, 1972's adult "classic" *Deep Throat* was an all-Florida production. Filmed in Fort Lauderdale with a budget of $24,000, the film earned more than $300 million worldwide. And that's just by those who admit to seeing it!

DID YOU KNOW?

Florida has long been a leading destination for gay men and women. And Fort Lauderdale in particular stands out for its gay-friendly attractiveness. In fact, the Greater Fort Lauderdale Convention and Visitor's Bureau has determined that the city ranks as "America's top gay resort area."

The Student and the Supermodel

Debra LaFave, a reading teacher in Temple Terrace, really wanted to make her students feel more comfortable. Unfortunately, she went about it in the wrong way, and in 2005, she was charged with several counts of having illegal sex with a minor. Born Debra Jean Beasley on August 28, 1980, LaFave had been a professional singer and model, and she liked to show off her body, especially at work. Not surprisingly, she was popular with the male students! In the book *Gorgeous Disaster,* written by Debra's ex-husband Owen LaFave, the teacher met her 14-year-old "beloved" at an after-school tag football game. All went smoothly until the boy's mother found out and contacted the police. After tape-recording the couple's conversations, the police ambushed and then arrested LaFave when she arrived at the boy's home.

Two separate sets of charges were filed, as the alleged criminal activity occurred in two different counties. LaFave soon revealed various reasons for her behavior, including manic depression and how she'd been raped by a schoolmate when she was 13.

Her defense attorney actually made things worse when he claimed that "to place Debbie into a Florida state women's penitentiary, to place an attractive young woman in that kind of hell hole, is like putting a piece of raw meat in with the lions."

On November 22, 2005, LaFave pleaded guilty and was sentenced to three years of house arrest and seven years of probation. On December 8, 2005, the second county's judge refused to accept a plea agreement calling for no prison time and set a trial date. However, the prosecutor dropped the charges. LaFave's teaching certificate was revoked, and she was sentenced to probation until 2015.

DID YOU  KNOW?

On September 29, 2006, former Backstreet Boy Nick Carter appeared on *Howard Stern* and claimed that he'd lost his virginity to LaFave, a fellow high school classmate!

FLORIDA'S ECONOMIC ENGINE

Sizzlin' Stats

Like the temperature, the economy of the Sunshine State is sizzling! Here's some proof:

☛ For the year 2005, Florida's gross state product was $596 billion.

☛ The state's total budget for the 2006–07 fiscal year is $70.8 billion, and the recommended operating budget is $56.1 billion.

☛ Florida's personal income was $30,098 per capita, ranking 26th nationally. From 1997 to 2004, the state's economy experienced an average annual growth rate of 4.2 percent, seventh among all states.

☛ Nationwide, Florida ranked an enviable sixth on the list of fastest growing private companies. Among the 25 companies representing the state, Airborne Health, based in Bonita Springs, came in second nation-wide for its three-year growth rate, an amazing 4673 percent!

☛ According to the Small Business Administration's 2006 report, when it comes to female-owned businesses, Florida ranks third after Nevada and Georgia.

☛ The state ranks fifth in being awarded Department of Defense contracts.

Median Earnings for Various Population Segments

☛ Female full-time, year-round workers: $29,352; 29th nationally

☛ Male full-time, year-round workers: $36,434; 39th nationally

☛ Family income: $49,461; 35th nationally

☛ Household income: $41,236; 36th nationally

Florida's Main Industries

The state's leading industries are tourism, agriculture and live-stock, phosphate mining, manufacturing, aviation/aerospace, construction, and health and biotechnology.

State Salary Scorecard

In Florida, it pays to be a good sport! Bobby Bowden, the Florida State University Seminoles football coach, is the state's highest-paid employee. Bowden, the winningest coach in college history, was paid $2,023,689.15 in 2006. But to be fair, his state salary was only $224,403.35; the remaining $1.8 million came from outside income. Bowden's biggest in-state rival, University of Florida football coach Urban Meyer, actually earned more. He made $2.1 million, but all of his earnings come from performance bonuses from private corporations and outside sources.

Billy Donovan, UF's basketball coach (and 2006 national championship winner), earned $179,173, with a minimum of $1.45 million in bonuses and a $60,000 expense account.

In general, the state's university presidents did well financially in 2006, averaging between $300,000 and $400,000 each. As for Florida's seven Supreme Court justices, they made $160,000 each in 2006. Women have come a long way in Florida, filling 11 of the top 50 slots for 2006. Meanwhile, the leader of the state, Governor Charlie Crist, earns $132,932 annually, ranking 969th on the list!

The Tax Facts

Searching for another reason to move to the Sunshine State? How about no personal income tax? According to the Tax Foundation research organization, Florida actually ranks among the lowest tax states, based on such factors as income, property and other state and local tax collections. How low? Well, in 2004, the state ranked 45th among all states, meaning only five states' residents had to pay less. The state's sales tax rate is only six percent, though local governments may charge certain businesses up to 1.5 percent.

Trade Secrets

Because of its unique geographical location and its international population, Florida—primarily the southeastern region—has become a center for international trade. In fact, 40 percent of all U.S. exports to Latin America pass through Florida. The overall value of these exports total more than $33 billion, and the state is responsible for 3.7 percent of the nation's total exports.

 Nationally, the state ranks 13th in manufacturing, employing 16,522 Floridians.

HOLIDAY HOTSPOT

The Tourism Capital

The beaches, the weather, the attractions, the beautiful people—as you've no doubt surmised, tourism is the largest segment of the state's economy. According to Visit Florida, the state's official source for travel planning:

☛ In 2006, 84.6 million total visitors traveled to Florida, compared to 83.6 million in 2005; 92 percent were from the U.S., while the other 8 percent were international visitors.

☛ The Department of Commerce ranks Florida second among all states for visiting foreigners, with Canadians making up the majority.

☛ The tourism industry brings in over $35 billion a year and employs more than one million Floridians.

☛ According to estimates, there are more than 370,000 hotel rooms in Florida.

DID YOU  KNOW?

In a recent poll of the nation's most hospitable cities, five of the top six slots were occupied by Florida cities: Miami, Fort Lauderdale, Orlando, Clearwater and St. Petersburg.

Camp Classic
Balmy temperatures, breathtaking views, thriving wildlife— who wouldn't want to camp out in the Sunshine State? Well, an estimated six million adventurers camp out here every year. To accommodate these brave individuals, Florida boasts more than 700 campgrounds that offer more than 100,000 campsites combined.

Searching for a scenic and satisfying car trip? In 2003, the

Society of American Travel Writers chose the Florida Keys Overseas Highway—the connection between the mainland and the islands—as one of the nation's 10 most beautiful drives.

FARMS AND FISH

Farming Factoids

☞ Agriculture is one of Florida's largest industries.

☞ For 2003, the Florida Department of Agriculture and Consumer Services ranked the state's leading crops as citrus fruits, sugarcane, tomatoes, bell peppers, snap beans, cucumbers, squash and grapefruit. In addition, the state produces large amounts of strawberries, potatoes, sweet corn, peanuts, watermelons, tangerines, cotton, cabbage, tobacco, blueberries, avocados and tangelos.

☞ As of 2003, Florida was home to 43,000 commercial farms.

☞ Florida farms occupy 10.1 million acres out of the state's nearly 35 million acres of land.

☞ In 2003, the state ranked ninth nationally in the value of farm products, with cash receipts of $6.45 billion.

☞ In 2002, Florida farms ranked eighth nationally in net farm income, with $1.8 billion.

☞ Florida is an agricultural trade partner with 100 nations, and this trade generates approximately $1.3 billion annually.

DID YOU KNOW?

If you love to crunch down on celery, you should give thanks to the Sunshine State. Florida ranks second nationally in celery production. From 1990 to 1994, Florida was responsible for 20 to 24 percent of the national celery acreage.

The Center of Citrus

When it comes to citrus fruits—especially oranges—Florida is national champ. This is the home of the Orange Bowl, after all!

☛ Citrus crops make up 18 percent of Florida farm sales.

☛ Florida's citrus growers produce 67 percent of the nation's entire citrus production.

☛ These growers cultivate 97.9 million trees on 748,555 acres.

☛ The state contributes 74 percent of the nation's supply and 13.9 percent of the world's entire supply of oranges.

☛ Florida produces 54 percent of the nation's grapefruits and 58 percent of the nation's tangerines.

They're Coming to America

Oranges have become synonymous with Florida's history, but they are actually imports! When Spanish explorers founded St. Augustine in 1565, they used the occasion to introduce oranges to the New World. The British were responsible for popularizing the fruit within the state.

The Sweet Life

In Florida, the sugar industry is one of the leading economic sectors, and the state is the nation's leader in sugarcane production. Boasting 600,000 acres of sugarcane fields and sugar mills, the state is responsible for an amazing 1.8 million tons of raw sugar, 21.4 percent of the nation's annual total! Statewide, the business of sugar generates average gross sales of over $2 billion and employs thousands of Floridians. All in all, in 2004, Florida's raw sugar crop was valued to be as much as $550 million!

Bugging Out

Florida has carved out a respectable reputation as an agricultural leader, but it hasn't all been bumper crops and good times. In August 1945, a 360-square-mile area of eastern Orange County was the site of the first large-scale testing of dichloro-diphenyl-trichloroethane (DDT). Although first created in 1874, the benefits of the synthetic chemical—dubbed the "wonder insecticide"—were not discovered until 1939. And, of course, it would be many years before the harmful effects on animals and humans were realized. DDT was remarkably effective at keeping bugs away from cattle and crops, but scientists soon found that houseflies were developing a tolerance to the chemical. Over the years, the chemical stuck around and infiltrated the food chain. Finally, in 1972, the U.S. government banned virtually all DDT use.

Part of a Well-Balanced Breakfast

In Florida, livestock production is essential to the economy. The state reported record gross receipts of over $1.5 billion in 2004! Indeed, Florida is a leading producer of many of the nation's dietary staples, such as milk, eggs, beef and poultry. For 2004, the state's dairies supplied almost 2.25 billion gallons of milk, totaling $432 million. Meanwhile, Florida's chicken and eggs receipts totaled $369 million.

A Major Economic "Cattle-lyst"

In 2004, Florida's cattle industry reported sales of more than $443 million. The state supplies 952,000 head a year, ranking 12th nationally and second among the southeastern states, after Kentucky. Most of Florida's cattle ranches are found near the Kissimmee River in Central Florida. In fact, Kissimmee's nickname is the "Cow Capital of Florida."

Fishing for Compliments

Florida is very waterlogged, with more than 2000 miles of shoreline and 11,000 miles of rivers, streams and other waterways. So, of course, fishing is a major economic force. The state's fishing industry, which employs more than 80,000 people, yields about $7.5 million in economic output and $4 million in fishing-related retail sales.

DID YOU KNOW?

The oceans off the coast of northeastern Florida are especially rich in shrimp. The waters near Amelia Island account for almost 80 percent of Florida's sweet Atlantic white shrimp supplies, while Fernandina's docks process two million pounds annually!

Maximum Horsepower

Florida has long relied on horses, whether for transportation, entertainment or even warfare. And horses mean big business! The state's horse industry produces goods and services valued at $2.2 billion annually. More than 200,000 Floridians are employed within the horse industry.

Florida, the Undisputed King of Phosphate

When was the last time you really thought about fertilizer? Are you aware that it's crucial to life on this planet? You see, plants require large amounts of three essential nutrients: nitrogen, phosphorus and potassium. Fertilizer replenishes these essential nutrients, even as they're used by existing crops.

So what does this have to do with Florida? Well, in the manufacturing process, a mineral known as phosphate is transformed into a water-soluble form of plant-nourishing fertilizer. And Florida, specifically the central region, is the undisputed leader in phosphate mining.

☛ Phosphate mining is the state's third-largest industry, employing about 6000 Floridians.

☛ Florida produces about 75 percent of the nation's phosphate and 25 percent of the world's supply.

☛ Phosphate and its related chemical products are the Port of Tampa's primary exports.

☛ In 2003, fertilizer was one of the state's leading export commodities, with a value of $1.3 billion.

☛ About 90 percent of all phosphate is used for fertilizer, and five percent is used for livestock feed supplements.

☛ The remaining five percent is used for other products, including film, light bulbs, vitamins, soft drinks, toothpaste, gum, optical glass, shaving cream, bone china, flame-resistant fabrics and detergents.

SKY HIGH

Into the great wide open,
Under them skies of blue,
Out in the great wide open,
A rebel without a clue.

–Tom Petty, "Into the Great Wide Open"

According to Enterprise Florida, Inc. (EFI), the state is a leader in the aviation and aerospace industries. Florida's aerospace industry really "took off" in 1962 with the construction of the NASA Merritt Island launch sites on Cape Canaveral, which included the Kennedy Space Center. Today, the Kennedy Space Center employs an estimated 15,000 people. It's also the home to the Astronaut Hall of Fame and the world's largest scientific building, the Vehicle Assembly Building at Launch Complex 39, which measures 716 feet long, 518 feet wide and 525 feet tall.

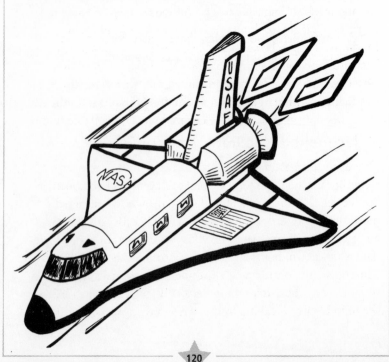

Other Spacey Facts

- Within the state, there are almost 1800 aviation and aerospace companies.

- The space industry represents $4.5 billion of Florida's economy.

- The state ranks third in the manufacturing of aircraft engines and parts.

- Florida ranks third in space, aerospace and aviation employment, with an estimated 83,000 workers.

- The state ranks fourth in manufacturing guided missiles and space vehicles.

- Florida ranks fourth in satellite communications.

DID YOU KNOW?

Among the 2004 inductees to the Astronaut Hall of Fame was Norman Thagard, a Florida native. Born July 3, 1943, in Marianna (though he considers Jacksonville his hometown), Thagard is a veteran of five space flights, having logged over 140 days in space. His career included a variety of roles such as mission specialist, payload commander and cosmonaut/researcher.

Jacqueline Cochran, Aviation Trailblazer

One of the greatest pilots in U.S. history—male or female—was Jacqueline Cochran Odlum. She broke not only the sound barrier, but the gender barrier as well! And along the way, she achieved more aviation records than anyone before her. Because she was an orphan (real name Bessie Lee Pittman), Cochran's exact birthdate is unknown, but she was likely born on May 11, 1908, in Muscogee. She overcame a childhood of poverty and dabbled in hairstyling, but after taking her first flying lesson in 1932, she found her new calling in life. After starting a successful

cosmetics company, Jacqueline pursued her passion for flying. In 1954, Jacqueline and her husband, Floyd Odlum, collaborated on her autobiography, *The Stars at Noon*. Among her aviation achievements, Jacqueline:

- won the Bendix Transcontinental Air Race in 1938;

- became a flight captain in the British Air Transport Auxiliary, training female pilots;

- organized and served as director of the United States Women's Air Force Service Pilots (WASPs);

- was awarded the Distinguished Service Medal in 1945;

- was commissioned a lieutenant colonel in the U.S. Air Force Reserve in 1948;

☛ set an altitude record of 55,253 feet;

☛ became the first woman to break the sound barrier on May 18, 1953, and later flew Mach 2;

☛ flew more than 1429 miles per hour, the fastest a woman had ever flown, in 1964;

☛ became the first woman to make a blind landing, in which pilots use only instruments for flying an aircraft, as the view is obstructed;

☛ was the first woman to take off from and land on an aircraft carrier;

☛ was the first woman to fly a fixed-wing jet aircraft across the Atlantic Ocean;

☛ was the first pilot to fly above 20,000 feet using an oxygen mask;

☛ became the first woman inducted into the National Aviation Hall of Fame in 1971;

☛ was the only woman to ever be President of the Federation Aeronautique Internationale (FAI), from 1958 to 1961. Founded in 1905, the FAI is a standard-setting and record-keeping body for aeronautics and astronautics. It is also the international governing body for air sports.

DID YOU KNOW?

A Miami pirate radio station called Da Streetz was found to be sending rap music into Miami International Airport cockpit radios. In similar Miami/airport/radio news, a station directing broadcasts towards Cuba was found to be disrupting airport communication with Latin music, Christian programs and anti-Castro programming.

TRANSPORTATION TIDBITS

Port Authority

☛ There are 14 deepwater ports located around Florida, including Pensacola, Miami, Panama City, Fort Lauderdale, Palm Beach, St. Petersburg, Fort Pierce, Tampa, Cape Canaveral, Bradenton, Sanford, Fernandina Beach and Jacksonville.

☛ Florida's ports service more than seven million cruise ship passengers each year.

☛ The busiest cruise ship port in the world is the Port of Miami (POM), which is frequented by 3.6 million cruise ship passengers annually. In 2005, POM serviced more than 30 ocean carriers and delivered more than one million cargo containers.

☛ Estimates show that Port Everglades in Fort Lauderdale may be the second busiest port in the world.

 **DID YOU KNOW?**

Florida's first graded road was Old Kings Road. Built in 1763, it was named for King George of England.

On the Right Track

In the 1800s, Dade County included the communities of current-day Broward and Palm Beach counties. However, this didn't sit well with residents living in the county's northernmost towns around Lake Okeechobee. Eventually, Dade's county seat was moved to Juno Beach. With the move came the need for a rail connection to link these population centers.

In October 1880, work began on the Jupiter & Lake Worth Railroad, also known as the "Celestial Railroad." The railroad chugged along for a few years but was finally sold at public auction in Jacksonville in June 1896. And while both Jupiter and Juno are still thriving today, the other "spacey" towns of Venus and Mars have entered the black hole of obscurity.

DID YOU KNOW?

MetroRail, an elevated train running 27.4 miles from North to South Miami, is one of the nation's largest transit systems and is the largest in Florida. Upon its completion, MetroRail, which cost $1 billion, was the single most expensive public transit project in U.S. history.

A MATTER OF LIFE AND DEATH

Life Sentences

When it comes to the state of health care in Florida, there's good news and bad news. To begin with, among statewide life expectancies, Florida comes in at number 21, with an average of 77.5 years.

Good: Collier County is among the counties with the highest life expectancy, at 81 years.

Bad: Union and Baker Counties are among the nation's 25 counties with the lowest life expectancy, with an average of 70.2 years.

Good: Florida's rate of infant mortality has steadily declined, from the 1955 rate of 29.7 per 1000 births to the 2002 rate of 7.5 per 1000! This drastic improvement is likely the result of such factors as better public health and prenatal, infant and child care programs.

Bad: According to the 2006 "America's Health Rankings" report, which was published jointly by the United Health Foundation, the American Public Health Association and the Partnership for Prevention, Florida ranked a depressing 41st out of all 50 states.

Good: In *U.S. News & World Report*'s annual list of America's best hospitals, eight Florida facilities made the cut!

Bad: Florida, like most states, is facing a health insurance crisis. In 2005, 3,593,320 men, women and children—20 percent of the population—were uninsured.

Cancer Rates on the Decrease

As you may have heard, cancer rates have been falling across the United States for the past two years, and Florida is no exception! According to the Florida Department of Health, the 2005 rate of cancer deaths in Florida was 223.8 per 100,000 people, compared to 224.3 in 2004 and 228.9 in 2003. The National Cancer Society attributes these falling rates to decades of research, as well as more effective levels of prevention, diagnosis and treatment of the disease. Men's deaths from cancer decreased the most for lung, prostate and colorectal cancer. Among women, deaths decreased the most for breast and colorectal cancer.

Welcome to God's Waiting Room

Florida has long had a reputation as a statewide retirement center, and guess what, the facts don't lie! Federal research shows that more than 80,000 residents are currently living in Florida nursing homes.

Is There a Doctor in the House?

Florida has more physicians and licensed practical nurses than the national average. In 2006, the state employed 55,858 non-federal (not employed by the government) physicians, while the whole nation employed 943,499. And statewide, there were 2.9 hospital beds available for every 1000 citizens. But Florida does have fewer dentists and physician assistants than the national average.

DID YOU KNOW?

In this day and age, an organ transplant is not that rare. But in 1995, a patient afflicted with a genetic disorder known as Gardner's Syndrome had to have all abdominal organs replaced. The patient needed to have seven organ transplants: kidney, pancreas, stomach, liver, large and small bowel and iliac artery (located in the pelvis).

Yellow Streak

In the early years of Florida's history, visitors and residents literally took their lives into their own hands! Florida's state health department was established in 1889. Unfortunately, it was a year too late; in 1888, a terrible outbreak of yellow fever hit the Jacksonville area hard. According to the Florida Entomology Laboratory at the University of Florida, of the city's 26,800 population, 10,000 fled. For those who remained, 5000 were sickened, and 400 died. Up until that year, yellow fever and cholera epidemics struck the state almost annually. In fact, yellow fever practically wiped out the entire population of St. Joseph in 1841!

DID YOU KNOW?

According to the Asthma and Allergy Foundation of America (AAFA), three million Floridians suffer from severe allergies. In addition, an estimated 900,000 people were afflicted with asthma in 2007, compared to the 740,000 individuals in 2000.

A YEARNING FOR LEARNING

Educational Achievements

In 2004, 14.1 percent of the state's adult population had not completed high school. Here is the good news:

☛ 84.5 percent of adult Floridians have completed high school, including equivalency

☛ 25.4 percent of adult Floridians have completed a bachelor's degree

☛ 9.1 percent of adult Floridians have completed an advanced degree

The Downside of Growth

Florida's fast-growing population may be good for the economy, but it means that an increasing proportion of the population has little or no education. Up to 5000 adults lacking adequate reading skills move into Florida each month, including migrants, refugees, dropouts and poverty-stricken families. Plus, the Florida Department of Education estimates that more than 1.5 million Floridians speak little or no English.

Read All About It!

The St. Augustine Free Public Library (1874) is the oldest in Florida. The state's largest library, the University of Florida Library, contains an excellent collection of works on the Caribbean. Florida has about 97 public library systems with nearly 500 library service outlets, including more than 30 bookmobiles, scattered throughout the state.

Going Old School

Floridians have the Spanish to thank for the state's school system, as they opened up the first schools in the 1600s. In the 1830s and 1840s, the state's efforts to establish a public school program proved unsuccessful. That is, until the state's 1868 constitution set aside provisions for a statewide system of public education.

HIGHER EDUCATION

College Collage

Florida now offers 169 degree-granting institutions, and it all started with Rollins College. Established in Winter Park in 1885, Rollins was founded by New England Congregationalists who wanted to give Floridians a taste of their own style of liberal arts education. Here's the timeline of when the state's biggest schools opened for business:

☛ Florida State University (FSU): founded in 1851, in Tallahassee, as the West Florida Seminary; in 1905, it became the Florida State College for Women, and in 1947, it became FSU

☛ University of Florida (UF): founded in 1853, in Gainesville, as the East Florida Seminary; became UF in 1906

☛ Florida Agricultural and Mechanical University (FAMU): founded in 1887, in Tallahassee

☛ University of Miami (UM): founded in 1925, in Coral Gables

☛ University of South Florida (USF): founded in 1956, in Tampa

☛ Florida Atlantic University (FAU): founded in 1961, in Boca Raton

☛ University of West Florida (UWF): founded in 1963, in Pensacola

☛ University of North Florida (UNF): founded in 1969, in Jacksonville

☛ Florida Gulf Coast University (FGCU): established in 1991, but first held classes in 1997, in Fort Myers

Medical Marvels

All of Florida's doctors have to come from somewhere! Studies show that 98 percent of all of new Florida medical school students are state residents. For those physicians practicing in the state's metropolitan areas, 12–22 percent went to a Florida medical school. Among the state's rural physicians, 12–30 percent went to a Florida medical school.

DID YOU  **KNOW?**

The first medical school in Florida opened in 1880. Known as the Tallahassee College of Medicine and Surgery, it eventually moved to Lake City. However, a few years later, it closed its doors forever.

More on the University of Florida

☛ The University of Florida (UF) in Gainesville is the third largest university in the United States, boasting 49,693 students; 34,612 are undergraduates and 15,081 are postgraduates.

☛ UF ranks second among all American institutions in the number of National Merit Scholar students enrolled, behind Harvard.

☛ UF has the eighth largest budget among all national universities—nearly $1.9 billion per year.

☛ According to *U.S. News & World Report*, the school's undergraduate program is currently ranked first in the state of Florida, 13th among American public universities and 47th among private and public universities.

☛ UF is the only Florida university to be selected as a member of the Association of American Universities.

☛ On the 2006 Academic Ranking of World Universities list, UF was ranked 53rd among world universities, based on research output and faculty awards.

FOR THE PEOPLE, BY THE PEOPLE

Politicians are like diapers. They both need changing regularly and for the same reason.

–Anonymous

Changing Teams

There was one thing the Democratic Party had always been able to count on, and that was Florida. Once upon a time, 68.5 percent of voters in the state were registered Democrats. But as the 20th century came to a close, the Republicans gradually took over. There was soon a Republican governor (more on that below), as well as Republican control of the state legislature, and half of the state's Senate seats. And that was one reason why the following occurred…

Election Rejection: Florida and the 2000 Election

The 2000 presidential election ended up being one of the closest in the nation's history. The tension was thick, as Democratic candidate Al Gore, vice president of the United States, and Republican candidate George W. Bush, governor of Texas, were almost neck and neck. And of course, the media didn't help at all.

Twice, the news outlets prematurely (and incorrectly) announced a winner in Florida, based on exit polls. With its huge population and number of electoral votes, Florida was considered a key swing state in presidential elections. It was soon obvious that both candidates needed the electoral votes of Florida to win. An entire month of court challenges and recounts ensued, with recounts (both hand- and machine-counted), lawsuits and angry allegations of both conflicts of interest and partisan, unethical

behavior. Many of these allegations were directed at Katherine Harris, Secretary of State for the State of Florida and co-chair for the Bush campaign.

Finally, the U.S. Supreme Court certified that Bush had won Florida by a margin of only 537 votes, thereby winning the presidency. However, Gore had actually received more votes than Bush nationwide. For only the third time in U.S. history, after the elections of 1876 and 1888, a president had won the vote in the Electoral College without receiving the majority of the popular vote. It ended up that the difference in the votes between Gore and Bush was less than one-tenth of one percent!

To this day, the Florida voting process is still a point of controversy. But it should be mentioned that had Gore won the popular vote in his home state of Tennessee, he would have won the election without Florida. So let's blame it all on Tennessee!

POLITICIANS IN PARADISE

Political "Harris"ment

No doubt inspired by her involvement in the 2000 presidential election, Katherine Harris decided to run for the Florida Senate in 2006. But, proving there is such a thing as karma, she met with embarrassing defeat. Virtually the entire Republican Party—including, ironically, Governor Jeb Bush, whose brother she allegedly helped to put in office—questioned her very ability and actually encouraged others to challenge her in the primary. Most of her staff deserted her, and her funds dwindled. She also angered many voters by claiming that she should be elected to "win back America for God." Not too surprisingly, Harris lost the election.

Nixon's Home Away From Home

Richard M. Nixon was no stranger to the Sunshine State and even owned a vacation home in Miami, which is today owned by real estate developer Edgardo Defortuna. Although the house has since been remodeled, the Presidential Seal remains on the front door.

And that's not all. After the humiliation of Watergate, Nixon gave his famous "I am not a crook" speech at Disneyworld on November 17, 1973.

DID YOU KNOW?

During his tenure as governor, from 1868–73, Harrison Reed was subjected to three separate impeachment inquiries!

Janet Reno, the Toughest Lawmaker in These Here Parts

A six-foot tall, no-nonsense legal wrecking ball, Janet Reno earned a place in history as the first female attorney general of the United States. In this role, she experienced amazing achievements and stinging criticisms, and she even became a fan favorite on *Saturday Night Live*.

The daughter of journalists, Reno (changed from Rasmussen) was born on July 21, 1938, in Miami. Reno served 15 years as Miami-Dade County's DA, and in that time, she won a record 103 death sentence convictions, though she was opposed to capital punishment. She was nominated as attorney general by President Bill Clinton after his first two nominees, Zoe Baird and Kimba Wood, were unable to be confirmed, because of revelations that both had previously employed illegal immigrants as nannies. Reno was confirmed as the 78th attorney general on March 11, 1993, and served throughout Clinton's presidency, making her the longest-serving attorney general since 1829. In 2002, she ran for governor of Florida but lost in the Democratic primary to Bill McBride.

Still, Janet Reno did earn a place in both Florida and U.S. history. She has long been an ardent crusader of programs aimed at child, spousal and drug abuse. In fact, she was immortalized in song by rap artist Anquette for her work to enforce child support payments. Reno dealt with criticisms over the handling of the Branch Davidian standoff in Waco, Texas, which resulted in the deaths of 82 people, including 20 children. She was also criticized for her handling of the deportation of Elián González.

Today, she travels the country giving speeches about the criminal justice system. And though she is afflicted with Parkinson's disease, causing her left hand to tremble, she still surfs the Atlantic Ocean in her kayak! Here are a few of Reno's career highlights:

- She created Florida's Drug Court program, which gives first-time offenders a second chance.

- As attorney general, she brought suit against Microsoft for violating the Sherman Antitrust Act.

- She solved the Centennial Olympic Park bombing and other bombings committed by Eric Rudolph.

- Reno contributed to the conviction of 21 of the Montana Freemen following an 81-day armed standoff.

- She was instrumental in the capture and conviction of the Unabomber.

- Reno was also responsible for the capture and conviction of Timothy McVeigh and Terry Nichols for the Oklahoma City bombing.

- She was also involved in the capture and conviction of Mir Aimal Kasi for the CIA headquarters shootings.

☛ She was responsible for the capture and conviction of Sheik Omar Abdel-Rahman and four conspirators in the World Trade Center bombing, resulting in life sentences.

The Gunrunning Governor

When it comes to Florida's history, even the politicians weren't boring! One of the state's most passionate and successful governors, Napoleon Bonaparte Broward, began his career running arms to Cuban freedom fighters. Naturally, this start led to a life in politics. Born in rural Duval County in 1857, Broward was elected sheriff of Duval County in 1890. He proved to be tough and honest, especially in his efforts to prevent vote-tampering. After being removed from office by the governor, Broward turned around and defeated the governor's appointee to win another term as sheriff in 1896. Broward was elected to the Florida House in 1900, and in 1904, he was elected governor.

Among his achievements as governor were the organization of a single governing board for Florida's colleges and universities, and the beginning of the efforts to drain and reclaim the Everglades. He strove for prison reform, better salaries for teachers, child labor laws and an eight-hour workday. Broward then won the race for the U.S. Senate but died, at the age of 53, before he could take office. Today, this Florida pioneer has one of the state's biggest and most populous counties named after him.

Walkin' Lawton Takes Office

I didn't come to stay. I came to make a difference.
–Lawton Chiles

Not only was Lawton Mainor Chiles Jr. one of Florida's most beloved governors, but he was also a proud supporter of cardiovascular fitness! Born in 1930 in Lakeland, Chiles had a successful 12-year term as a state legislator. Once it ended, he decided to run for the U.S. Senate. But Chiles was still considered an unknown throughout the state. So, in 1970, Lawton came up with a truly inspired and health-boosting public relations campaign—he set off on a 91-day, 1003-mile walk across Florida, from the Panhandle to the Keys. The journey enabled him to meet the people and to take in both the state's beauty and its problems. Chiles succeeded in earning recognition, and his down-home political style connected with voters. He easily won the election and earned his nickname, "Walkin' Lawton."

Elected governor of Florida in 1990 and 1994, Chiles scored some major victories even though he was at the mercy of the state's Republican Congress. His accomplishments included:

☛ winning a landmark $11.3 billion settlement against the tobacco industry;

☛ winning approval for a $2.7 billion statewide school construction program;

☛ earning a reputation as an advocate for health care and children's issues;

☛ establishing the National Commission for Prevention of Infant Mortality;

☛ creating the Florida Department of Elder Affairs;

☛ establishing Florida's Healthy Start program, which provides cut-rate prenatal and infant care to low-income mothers across the state (since the program's inception, Florida's infant mortality rate has dropped 20 percent);

☛ appointing a Governor's Commission on Education to examine the statewide school system; and

☛ appointing five of the seven Justices to the Florida Supreme Court, and jointly appointing a sixth Justice.

When Chiles was running for re-election in 1994, his Republican opponent, Jeb Bush, was in front for most of the campaign. But Lawton turned the tide at the last minute by turning on his Southern charm. When a reporter asked him some questions about the losing campaign, Chiles responded with a now-famous line: "The old he-coon walks just before the light of day." This old Southern saying, which refers to the oldest and wisest raccoon in a pack, won over many Floridians who knew that Chiles spoke from the heart. It also spotlighted Bush's inexperience and habit of reading from a script. Chiles, who scored a narrow victory, showed his thanks by wearing a coonskin cap on election night.

OTHER ISSUES

Flight of the Canadian Snowbirds

Every year, more and more people flock to Florida's borders, and every year, fewer and fewer leave. According to a University of Florida study, the state's population fluctuates by nearly 20 percent, swelled by the arrival of the winter visitors known as "snowbirds." The Canadian Snowbird Association defines a snowbird as someone who spends 31 or more nights in a southern destination. The study showed that in winter 2005, an estimated 818,000 snowbirds spent at least one month in Florida, while in July 2005, an estimated 313,000 elderly Floridians spend at least 30 consecutive days somewhere else.

When it comes to visitors from outside the United States, Canada is the Florida's leading international partner, as well as the undisputed importer of snowbirds to the Sunshine State. And the relationship goes deeper than just tourism. Studies show that:

☞ Canada is Florida's number one source of inbound tourism.

☞ Canada is Florida's number one source of foreign direct investment.

☞ Canada is Florida's number two destination of Florida exports, after Brazil.

☞ Canadians are responsible for an estimated 90,000 jobs in Florida or about 1.3 percent of the state's entire employment.

☞ In 2003, 219,500 Canadians visited Florida, with 58.7 percent spending 60 nights or more, and more than 20 percent spending 91 nights or more.

☞ Canadians are the state's best source for foreign commercial real estate investment, with a total of $3.6 billion invested as of 2001.

The Canada-Florida snowbird phenomenon is nothing new, but it used to be much more violent! During the 1870s, the state government ruled that dockworkers had to live in Florida for six months before they could be hired. This proclamation led to outbreaks of violence, such as a fight in Pensacola in the 1870s between dockworkers from both nations. However, when the locals and the state realized how much money the Canadian newcomers were bringing in, they welcomed their new neighbors with open arms!

Environmental Mayhem

In 2002, weather-related disasters cost Florida almost $263 million in losses. According to James O'Brien, Florida's state climatologist, global warming will have a number of destructive effects on Florida, including an increased number and fiercer intensity of hurricanes; increases in forest fires; dying coral reefs; retreating and eroding shorelines; saltwater intrusion into inland freshwater aquifers; and warmer air and sea-surface temperatures. The biggest threat is likely the projected rising sea levels. Along the coast, the sea level is expected to rise six to 10 times faster than the average rate over the past 3000 years, meaning that the sea level may rise 20 inches by 2100!

It's in the Air

Florida is the fifth largest producer of greenhouse gases in the country. Studies show that in 2001, residents breathed unhealthy air on 14 days. In studies conducted by the Southern Alliance for Clean Energy (SACE), it was found that coal-fired power plants emit sulfur dioxide pollution in the form of fine particles. And when it comes to fine particle pollution, the SACE found that in 2002, Florida ranked third for hospitalizations (1367); fifth for heart attacks (2145); and third for total deaths (1416). In addition, the SACE found that Florida ranks fifth in the nation for carbon dioxide emissions, with its power plants contributing more than 104 million tons of carbon dioxide annually.

Water Worries

As for Florida's waterways, in 2002, a fish consumption advisory for mercury pollution was given for all of the state's rivers, lakes and coasts. In addition, the state is dealing with such obstacles as nonstop dredging and draining, diverting of freshwater and declining water quality. According to the Sierra Club, approximately 50 percent of Florida's estuaries—indicators of freshwater quality—appear to be showing signs of impairment for both human and aquatic life use, while 31 percent of the state's freshwater rivers and streams are now impaired or unusable for aquatic resources. About 50 percent of all Florida wetlands have already been destroyed.

Superfund to the Rescue!

Superfund is America's premiere environmental law, forcing polluters to clean up the nation's most contaminated toxic waste sites. And in Florida, there are 51 sites on Superfund's National Priority List. In 2004, Florida taxpayers paid an estimated $73.6 million to clean up abandoned toxic waste sites. And here's a little tidbit: the U.S. Department of Defense is responsible for seven of the state's Superfund toxic waste sites.

MUSEUM MUSINGS

Latino and Hispanic Art

Located in Coral Gables, the Florida Museum of Hispanic and Latin American Art is renowned as the first and only museum in the United States that is dedicated to the preservation, diffusion and promotion of Hispanic and Latin American art.

 Sanibel boasts the world's only mollusk-themed museum, which is home to two million shells. The city's beaches are considered to be some of the best in the world for shell collecting. In fact, the position assumed by shell collectors, standing with legs spread apart and bent at the waist, is known as the "Sanibel Stoop."

Not So Ladylike

In May and June 1996, Sarasota's Donn Roll Contemporary Museum showcased artist Charon Luebbers' Menstrual Hut. This six-by-six-by-five-foot isolation booth symbolized the loneliness that menstruating women are subjected to in our society. The exhibit featured 28 paintings that were created in a truly unique manner: every day for a month, Luebbers pressed her face into the daily discharge produced via her cycle!

Cartoon Art

Beetle Bailey creator Mort Walker took a gamble on the public's love of comic strips and opened the National Cartoon Museum in 1974 in Greenwich, Connecticut. The museum, which was the first established to preserve and exhibit cartoon art, underwent a name change, becoming the International Museum of Cartoon Art. By 1992, the collections grew so large that Walker moved the entire museum to a 52,000-square-foot facility in Boca Raton. For a decade, the museum attracted fans from all over the world. However, financial difficulties soon led to the museum's relocation to New York City.

An Alternative Archive

The Key West Gay & Lesbian Museum & Archive, housed in the Gay and Lesbian Community Center, opened in June 2006. Visitors will find such exhibits as Tennessee Williams' typewriter and a collection of memorabilia and papers of Richard A. Heyman, Key West's former mayor and one of the nation's first openly gay mayors until his 1994 AIDS-related death.

DID YOU  KNOW?

Florida is a truly cultured state. Ten of the state's cities support symphony orchestras, and five have opera companies. There are more than 100 dance companies. In addition, Florida has more than 100 professional and amateur theater groups.

FINE ART IN FLORIDA

Plastic Fantastic

Proving that tackiness knows no bounds, may we present…the Surrounded Islands! In May 1983, two artists, Christo (real name Hristo Yavashev) and his wife Jeanne-Claude (full name Jeanne-Claude Denat de Guillebon) had the vision to surround 11 islands in Miami's Biscayne Bay with almost two million square feet of pink polypropylene plastic. The completed island art would be on display for two weeks, before all of the materials were stripped away and completely recycled. Why was this done? Because it was art!

Overcoming plenty of arguments, especially of the environmental kind, the project was eventually completed on May 7, 1983. The massive project required the placement of anchors around the island and underwater, as well as the construction of floatation booms. Five hundred people contributed to the project, and it was said that cleaning crews removed as much as 40 tons of garbage from the 11 islands. Ironically, this left the islands cleaner than before the exhibit! In the end, Christo and Jeanne-Claude's artwork cost an estimated $3 million, but it did boost tourism.

DID YOU KNOW?

Key West was the birthplace and home of Mario Sanchez, one of America's greatest folk artists. Born in 1908 to Cuban immigrants, Sanchez gained fame for his colorful and historically accurate painted wood carvings of old Key West. In 1961, Cary Grant, who was in town filming *Operation Pettycoat,* stopped by and bought a couple of Sanchez's carvings for both himself and his friend, Spencer Tracy.

Bok in the Saddle

In the charming town of Lake Wales, you will find one of Florida's most tranquil attractions, the Bok Sanctuary. This haven for beauty and serenity was founded by Edward W. Bok, a noted philanthropist and publisher of *The Ladies' Home Journal*. Although he was a passionate crusader for many social causes, the environment was especially important to Bok. In 1921, while on vacation in the Lake Wales Ridge area, Bok fell in love with Florida's natural beauty. He decided then and there to preserve the area's splendor and wildlife with a bird sanctuary.

Bok bought the land and commissioned famous landscape architect Frederick Law Olmsted Jr. to realize his vision. A variety of bushes and trees were planted, and a reflection pool was constructed, which is one of the most popular attractions to this day. But Bok knew that his retreat needed something else—the pleasing sounds of the carillons (bells) from his childhood in the Netherlands. He recruited renowned architect Milton B. Medary to erect a beautiful tower to be the focal point of the sanctuary. A large carillon would serve as the crown of the 205-foot tower, which was dedicated on February 1, 1929.

Today, visitors flock to the unique and ear-pleasing appeal—the tower's 53 bells chime every 30 minutes—of the "Singing Tower." The Bok Sanctuary is a popular Central Florida attraction and is also a retreat from the hustle and bustle of the rat race. Visitors can take in a sumptuous garden of lush plant life and native Floridian wildlife, as well as the majesty of tower itself.

A Unique Type of Bird Conservation

Noted naturalist John James Audubon was also renowned for his paintings of exotic birds, especially those found in the Florida Keys. However, Audubon had a strange method of preserving avian life; he killed the birds, ran wires through their bodies and then arranged them in poses! A big flamingo fan, Audubon once killed one, had it preserved in rum and then shipped it to his Charleston studio. Only then did he finish sketching the bird.

ARCHITECTURE

Boca Bonanza

Considered the father of the Spanish Revival style of architecture, Addison Mizner was responsible for changing the look of Palm Beach County and Florida in general. And he did it all without any formal training! A California native, Mizner moved to Palm Beach to improve his health. Once in the Sunshine State, his creative juices flowed, and in the spring of 1925, he founded the Mizner Development Corp. Mizner focused on transforming a sleepy, rural hamlet known as Boca Raton into a luxurious resort community.

And he definitely succeeded! Mizner purchased over 1500 acres (more than two square miles), including two miles of beach, and soon, other developers flocked to the growing city. Unfortunately, the land bust hit him hard, and Mizner was left bankrupt in 1927. He died of a heart attack in 1933 at the age of 61. But his architectural contributions to the area were well received, and an 11-foot-tall statue was erected in Boca Raton in March 2005 in his honor.

The Wright Stuff

Florida Southern College, located in Lakeland, is home to the world's largest collection of Frank Lloyd Wright architecture, known as *Child of the Sun*. As these buildings are so historically valuable, the entire campus is designated a National Historic Site.

LITERATURE MAJOR

Don't Mess with Papa

Sure, Ernest Hemingway had a great love for Key West's bars and women, but what about his writing efforts? Hemingway arrived in Key West in April 1928, and it was this southernmost city that really got his creative juices flowing. While a resident, he wrote some of his most classic works, including *Death in the Afternoon, The Green Hills of Africa*, and a short story, "The Short Happy Life of Francis Macomber." Plus, he worked on parts of *A Farewell to Arms*.

Embracing the Key West lifestyle, "Papa" Hemingway had a great time writing, drinking, boxing and fishing. Then in 1935, a tourist guidebook published a map featuring Key West tourist attractions, including Hemingway's home. The author was so angry about losing his anonymity that he hired a local brick-layer to build a red brick wall around his house. That wall is still standing today.

"Book 'em": A Selection of Florida Authors

- Dave Barry: Born July 3, 1947, in Armonk, New York, Barry has emerged as a leading chronicler of all of the craziest, grossest and most ridiculous behavior in South Florida. The former *Miami Herald* columnist is a Pulitzer Prize–winning humorist, as well as a bestselling author. Oh, and he's also an expert on boogers, farts, stupid dogs, poorly educated teenagers, explosions and bad driving habits—all the stuff that makes Florida the state it is!

- Patricia Cornwell: Born Patricia Carroll Daniels on June 9, 1956, in Miami, Cornwall is the author of the bestselling "Dr. Kay Scarpetta" series.

- Tim Dorsey: Born in 1961, in Indiana, he moved to Riviera Beach as a one-year-old. He is the author of the hysterical and historical *Serge Storms* comedy/crime drama series. He is also a former reporter for the *Tampa Tribune*.

- Carl Hiaasen: Born March 12, 1953, in Plantation, Hiaasen is a well-respected investigative reporter for the *Miami Herald*, as well as a bestselling author. He is a champion of preserving Florida's natural beauty and limiting construction and corruption within the state. His books are classified as "environmental thrillers." All told, he has written 11 mega-popular novels, three collaborative efforts, two children's books, including 2002's *Hoot*, which was made into a movie, and various non-fiction works, and he has had his *Herald* columns made into collections.

- Zora Neale Hurston: Born January 7, 1891, in Notasulga, Alabama, Hurston is celebrated by Floridians for her literary efforts, such as her 1928 essay, "How It Feels To Be Colored Me," which spoke of her childhood in Eatonville. Her biggest success was her 1937 novel *Their Eyes Were Watching God*, which was made into a TV movie in 2005 starring Halle Berry. On January 28, 1960, Hurston died in poverty and was buried in an unmarked grave in Fort Pierce. However, in 1973, her grave was reclaimed and marked, heralding the rediscovery of Hurston's legacy. Her Fort Pierce home was declared a National Historic Landmark, and today the city holds annual events and a festival at the end of April called Zora Fest.

☛ James Weldon Johnson: Born June 17, 1871, in Jacksonville, he was renowned as an author, poet, early civil rights activist and prominent figure in the Harlem Renaissance. Johnson was one of the first African-American professors at New York University. He died on June 26, 1938.

☛ Marjorie Kinnan Rawlings: Born August 8, 1896, in Washington, DC, Rawlings is now recognized as one of the greatest champions of Florida and its limitless potential. Over the years, Rawlings became enamored of the state's natural beauty, which greatly influenced her 1938 novel *The Yearling*, about a boy and his adopted fawn. The book won a Pulitzer Prize and was made into a hit movie. Rawlings died in 1953, but her legacy has been well preserved. A dormitory at the University of Florida—where she taught creative writing—bears her name, and Marjorie Kinnan Rawlings Historic State Park was built on the site of her former land in Cross Creek.

☛ Jeffrey Shaara: Born 1952 in New Brunswick, New Jersey, but raised in Tallahassee (he's a graduate of FSU), Shaara is the author of bestselling works of historical fiction, including 1974's *The Killer Angels* and 1991's *For Love of the Game* (which became a Kevin Costner movie).

☛ Lillian Smith: Born December 12, 1897, in Jasper, she is the author of 1944's *Strange Fruit*.

☛ Randy Wayne White: Born in 1952 in Ohio, White has become a Florida fixture. His bestselling *Doc Ford* series of hard-bitten, southwestern Florida-based crime fiction has won him droves of fans. White is active in South Florida's civic affairs and is also involved with Doc Ford's Sanibel Rum Bar & Grill on Sanibel Island.

DID YOU 🏠 **KNOW?**

Dave Barry and fellow authors Stephen King, Amy Tan, Ridley Pearson, Mitch Albom, Kathi Goldmark, Roy Blount Jr., Barbara Kingsolver and Matt Groening (creator of *The Simpsons*) have long been performing together in a rock band known as the Rock Bottom Remainders. The abilities of the group, which plays for charity, were aptly summed up by Barry when he said that the members "are not musically skilled, but they are extremely loud."

MUSIC TO OUR EARS

Attack of the Boy Bands!

In the late 1990s, the depressing and angry sounds of grunge were sliding down the charts. But then suddenly the nation, and soon the world, came under the insidious and infectious influence of an all-consuming threat. And Orlando, Florida, was ground zero for this epidemic!

Thanks to the efforts of Lou Pearlman, former pilot and guitarist turned band manager, the airwaves were monopolized by tunes about puppy love and busting moves. Record stores and virtually every mainstream publication were soon sporting images of such artists as *NSync, the Backstreet Boys, O Town and LFO. And it wasn't just a boy's club; teen queens like Britney Spears, Christina Aguilera and Mandy Moore also began their musical careers in Orlando. These artists sold phenomenally well: the Backstreet Boys sold 65 million records worldwide, and *NSync sold over 56 million records. In fact, *NSync's 2001 album *No Strings Attached* sold 2.4 million copies in its first week of release alone, which is still the biggest first week album sales tally in music history!

A Selected List of Florida-Themed Songs
Standards

"Moon Over Miami"
"Florida Among the Palms"
"Miami Beach Rumba"
"The Orange Blossom Special"
"Charming Florida"
"Down Where the Suwanee River Flows"
"Florida Glide Waltz"
"Florida Moon"
"In Dear Old Sunny Florida"
"I've Got the Swanee River Flowing Thru My Veins"
"My Florida Home"
"Florida Rag"

Modern

"Moving to Florida," Butthole Surfers
"Mainline Florida," Eric Clapton
"Floridays," Jimmy Buffett
"Deep Down in Florida," Muddy Waters
"Florida Twist," Bill Haley
"St. Pete Florida Blues," Ray Charles
"Florida Blues," Jim Eanes & His Shenandoah Valley Boys
"Road to Florida," Mekons
"Miami 2017 (I've Seen the Lights Go Out on Broadway)," Billy Joel
"Via Miami," Deep Purple
"Tallahassee Lassie," Jan and Dean
"King Kong Goes to Tallahassee," Bruce Cockburn
"Tallahassee," Bing Crosby
"Talk Me Out of Tampa," Joe Nichols
"Tampa," Gipsy Kings
"Jacksonville Kid," Lynyrd Skynyrd
"Key West Intermezzo (I Saw You First)," John Mellencamp
"Key West," Village People

"Gainesville Rock City," Less Than Jake
"Fort Lauderdale Chamber of Commerce," Elvis Presley

Assorted Tunes Called "Florida" By:

Aberdeen
Diplo
Hank Gandy
MOFRO
Bertie Higgins
Vic Chesnutt
Patty Griffin

Assorted Tunes Called "Miami" By:

Taking Back Sunday
John Mellencamp
Will Smith
Sublime

Pat Boone

In spite of his side trip into heavy metal, Charles Eugene Patrick Boone has carved out a squeaky-clean and triumphant career as a singer, actor, motivational speaker, TV star and conservative political commentator. Born June 1, 1934, in Jacksonville, Boone initially gained fame by covering African-American R&B hits for white audiences. He eventually became the second most popular singer of the late 1950s, after Elvis.

Harry Wayne Casey

You probably know him better as "KC," and along with his party-friendly Sunshine Band, he has sold an estimated 75 million albums worldwide. Harold Wayne Casey was born on January 31, 1951, in Opa-Locka, and he and his band were instrumental in founding and perfecting the funky, tropical and energetic "Miami Sound." Along with the Beatles, KC and the Sunshine Band are the only band to have four number one singles in one year.

Debbie Harry

As the singer and front woman for Blondie, this ex-Playboy bunny and her band have sold an estimated 40 million albums. Born in Miami in 1945, Harry has gone on to a successful career as a solo act and an actress. Blondie was inducted into the Rock and Roll Hall of Fame in 2006.

Gram Parsons

Revered for his tenure with two classic rock groups, the Byrds and the Flying Burrito Brothers, Parsons also earned respect for his solo success. Today, Parsons is considered a founding father of both the country rock and alt-country movements. Born Cecil Ingram Connor III on November 5, 1946, in Winter Haven, Parsons was multitalented as a singer, songwriter, guitarist and pianist. Unfortunately, Parsons eventually succumbed to a drug addiction and reportedly died of an alcohol/morphine overdose at the age of 26. But his legacy was preserved for music lovers, as evidenced by a 2004 issue of *Rolling Stone*. In its "100 Greatest Artists of All Time," Parsons was ranked 87th.

Vanilla Ice

Born Robert Matthew Rip Van Winkle on October 31, 1968, in Miami Lakes, Vanilla Ice achieved explosive fame in the early 1990s to become one of the most commercially successful rappers ever. And to the amazement of the entire hip-hop community, his big hit, "Ice Ice Baby" held the record of becoming the first number one rap single in history, and it held the spot for 16 weeks! Vanilla Ice was on top of the world…for a few months. Then his 1991 cinematic debut *Cool As Ice* bombed, and his rap career plummeted. He went on to unsuccessfully recreate himself as a "gangsta" rapper, and later, a reality TV star. Today, he still calls South Florida his home and is working on his next album.

Tom Petty

Born October 20, 1950, Gainesville's favorite (non-athletic) son has been piling up critical and commercial successes for 30 years. Along the way—both solo and with his band, the Heartbreakers— he's sold an estimated 50 million albums! Petty has earned 16 Grammy Award nominations and has won three. He was also a proud member of the classic supergroup, the Traveling Wilburys. In 2002, Tom Petty and the Heartbreakers were inducted into the Rock and Roll Hall of Fame.

Suicide is Not a "Petty" Crime!

Have you heard the urban legend about Tom Petty's hit song "American Girl"? Many think that the tune was inspired by a female student at the University of Florida who committed suicide. Rumors persist that she jumped to her death from the balcony of her dormitory room in Gainesville's Beatty Towers. And it's understandable why so many believe the rumor is true. After all, Petty is a Gainesville native, and the song's lyrics reference Highway 441, which runs past the college.

But upon closer inspection, you find some holes in the theory. For instance, nowhere in the song are Gainesville, Beatty Towers or the University of Florida mentioned. And as any UF alumnus is aware, not only do the Beatty Towers have no balconies, but the rooms' windows are too small and awkwardly positioned for anyone to jump from. Petty himself addressed the suicide rumor in an interview. According to the singer, not only is the rumor completely untrue, but the lyrics had nothing to do with Florida at all! Actually, the song was inspired by a freeway outside the southern California apartment building where he was living when he wrote the song.

Luther Campbell

Known as "Uncle Luke" or "Luke Skywalker," Luther Campbell has emerged as a leading figure in South Florida's free speech efforts, whether he wanted to or not! Campbell was born December 22, 1960, in Miami, and went on to gain fame and notoriety with the 2 Live Crew.

Campbell's Scoop: The 2 Live Crew Goes to Court

Although the group sold millions of albums and raced up the charts, their X-rated lyrics had the Religious Right up in arms, and soon, the law got involved. In 1990, the Broward County courts ruled that there was probable cause that the band's *As Nasty as They Wanna Be* album was obscene under state law. Campbell fought back and sued over First Amendment issues, but the album was again ruled to be obscene by the state federal court. In 1992, the Florida state court's ruling was reversed by the 11th U.S. Circuit Court of Appeals in Georgia. Today, Campbell is proud of his musical legacy and is considered a leading figure in the red-hot Miami rap scene.

More Florida-Born Hit-Makers

☛ Arthur "Blind" Blake, blues singer and guitarist: Born circa 1893 in Jacksonville; known as the King of Ragtime Guitar

☛ Julian "Cannonball" Adderley, jazz saxophonist: Born September 15, 1928, in Tampa

☛ Sam Moore, of Sam & Dave fame: Born October 12, 1935, in Miami

☛ Gary U.S. Bonds (Gary Anderson): Born June 6, 1939, in Jacksonville

☛ Jackie Moore, R&B/disco singer: Born 1946, in Miami

☛ Rick Dees (Rigdon Ogden Dees III), DJ, "Disco Duck" creator: Born March 14, 1950, in Jacksonville

☛ James MacDonough, former Iced Earth and Megadeth bass player: Born April 3, 1970, in Jacksonville

☛ Trick Daddy (Maurice Young), rapper: Born 1975, in Miami

☛ Mase (Mason Durrell Betha), rapper: Born August 27, 1977, in Jacksonville

☛ Pitbull (Armando Christian Pérez), rapper: Born January 15, 1981, in Miami

Creed

Formed in Tallahassee in 1995, this "Pearl Jam-esque" quartet blended grunge-like tunes with spirituality and sold an estimated 25 million albums in the U.S. They were long considered Christian rock, which they denied. Eventually their singer, Scott Stapp, left the band and began his solo career, while the other band members launched a successful new group, Alter Bridge.

Limp Bizkit

This Jacksonville combo was considered to be a leading force in the formation—along with Korn and the Deftones—of "nu metal," a mix of heavy metal and rap. And around the end of the 20th century, they were one of the planet's most successful groups, selling more than 30 million albums worldwide. Nevertheless, the band has never been critically accepted: when reviewing their 2003 album *Results May Vary,* one critic, Stephen Thomas Erlewine of www.allmusic.com, wrote that lead singer Fred Durst was the "worst front man in the history of rock." Ouch!

matchbox twenty

In 1996, this Orlando-based rock band exploded on the scene and went on to sell 39 million copies worldwide of their three albums. Lead singer and pianist Rob Thomas has found solo success as well.

38 Special

In 1975, Donnie Van Zant, younger brother of Ronnie Van Zant (of Lynyrd Synyrd), formed this Jacksonville band, which he named after the .38 Special pistol. During the 1980s, the group scored hit after hit, blending Southern rock with a more straightforward rock sound.

The Allman Brothers

Formed in Jacksonville in 1969, these classic rock heroes have long been praised for their epic jam sessions and touring. Tragedy struck when one of the founders, guitarist Duane Allman, was killed in a motorcycle accident in 1971. But the band overcame their loss, and over the years, they won a Grammy, were inducted into the Rock and Roll Hall of Fame and made it on to the *Rolling Stone*'s "100 Greatest Artists of All Time" list at number 55. Plus, they earned 11 gold and five platinum albums.

Lynyrd Skynyrd

Formed in 1964, this Southern rock band has a lot in common with the Allman Brothers. Like the Allmans, they had to overcome tragedy—actually, it was one of the worst catastrophes in the history of rock!

In 1977, the band was flying to a show at Louisiana State University in Baton Rouge, when their plane crashed near a forest in McComb, Mississippi. The crash killed the band's leader, vocalist and primary songwriter Ronnie Van Zant, guitarist/vocalist Steve Gaines, his sister Cassie, also a vocalist, road manager Dean Kilpatrick and both pilots. The rest of the passengers suffered a wide range of injuries, some serious.

However, the band survived and is now considered to be one of the most commercially and critically successful Southern rock groups of all time. Lynyrd Skynyrd has sold more than 20 million albums, and in 2006, the band was inducted into the Rock and Roll Hall of Fame. Oh, and the band's name comes from an ex-gym teacher, Leonard Skinner, who had at one time suspended some of the band members for having long hair. Apparently not a fan, Skinner said, "You boys ain't never gonna amount to nothin'."

The King of the Parrotheads

When the subject of Florida music comes up, there's always one name that surfaces—Jimmy Buffett. Born on December 25, 1946, in Pascagoula, Mississippi, Buffett has definitely earned the right to be considered a son of Key West and Florida in general. With or without his fan-favorite Coral Reefer Band, Buffett has experienced great success, which began with 1970's *Down to Earth*. However, that's only the tip of the iceberg; he's also emerged as a successful author, restauranteur and business leader. And to his legion of dedicated fans, known as Parrotheads, the performer can do no wrong.

- ☞ Jimmy Buffet began his career as a correspondent for *Billboard* magazine in Nashville.

- ☞ Buffett's 1977 hit song "Margaritaville" reached number eight on the *Billboard* charts; the song helped to establish his beach-loving reputation.

- ☞ He has earned seven gold albums, four platinum albums and two double platinum albums and has been nominated for two Grammy Awards.

- ☞ Today, Buffett prefers to play only on Tuesdays, Thursdays and Saturdays, explaining the title of his 1999 live album, *Buffett Live: Tuesdays, Thursdays, Saturdays.*

- ☞ Buffett is the owner of the Margaritaville Café restaurant chain.

- ☞ Buffett has written three number one *New York Times* bestsellers: *Tales from Margaritaville, Where Is Joe Merchant?* and *A Pirate Looks at Fifty.* His latest book, *A Salty Piece of Land,* was released in 2004 and quickly became a bestseller.

- ☞ He's one of only seven authors to have reached number one on the *Times'* fiction and nonfiction lists.

- ☞ Buffett earns an estimated $60 to $70 million a year from his album sales, touring and restaurants.

Attention, Rock Stars!
Be on Your Best Behavior, or Else!

As the Righteous Brothers song goes, "If there's a rock and roll heaven, then you know they've got a hell of a band!" Today's Florida may be a hotspot for the latest tunes and hit-makers, but in past decades, the Sunshine State caused endless amounts of grief for the biggest names in music.

In 1956, Elvis came to sing and do his thing in Jacksonville. However, his brand of pelvic thrusting didn't sit well with a local judge. The indignant judge actually came to the show with his band of "morally upright citizens" and carefully monitored every movement. After the very toned-down show, the good judge proceeded to lecture Elvis on the rules of proper behavior. Needless to say, Presley held a grudge towards the judge!

In August 1969, Janis Joplin was at the height of her popularity, having given a titanic performance at Woodstock. Now, Janis was no angel, and she was pretty fond of booze and drugs, but she could still put on a great show. At a Tampa concert on November 16, 1969, the audience was grooving to her music; so much so that a policeman climbed onstage with a bullhorn to warn the dancing crowd to clear the aisles. An outraged and sloshed Janis stopped singing and began screaming obscenities at the cops. The men in blue allowed her to finish the show, then arrested her onstage. She was charged with two counts of public use of profanity and fined $200. Janis Joplin was found dead of a heroin overdose just four months later.

The Doors' charismatic front man Jim Morrison was no stranger to public displays of wild behavior. But in 1969, he displayed a little too much at the Dinner Key Auditorium in Coconut Grove, Miami, when he exposed himself onstage. A warrant was issued for the Florida native (born in Melbourne, in 1943) on one felony count of lewd and lascivious behavior and three misdemeanor counts of indecent exposure, open profanity and drunkenness. Morrison turned himself in to the FBI on April 4, 1969, and on November 9, 1969, he pleaded not guilty. The trial began on August 12, 1970, and on September 20, 1970, Morrison was found guilty on two of the misdemeanor charges. Judge Goodman sentenced Jim to six months of hard labor and a $500 fine. His lawyer filed an immediate appeal. Until the appeal could be heard, Jim would be free on a $50,000 bond. Jim Morrison drowned in a Parisian bathtub on July 3, 1971, before his legal problems could be resolved.

Finally, back in 1986, Richard Manuel, former pianist for the classic rock ensemble the Band, was found dead in his Winter Park hotel room. Apparently, Manuel had hanged himself.

LIGHTS, CAMERA, ACTION!

Actors Born in Florida:

☛ Wayne Brady: Born June 2, 1972, in Orlando; *Whose Line Is It Anyway*, *The Wayne Brady Show*

☛ Delta Burke: Born July 30, 1956, in Orlando; *Designing Women*, *1st & Ten*

☛ Faye Dunaway: Born January 14, 1941, in Bascom; *Bonnie and Clyde*, *Chinatown*, *Mommie Dearest*; won an Oscar for *Network*

☛ Carla Gugino: Born August 29, 1971, in Sarasota; *Spin City*, *Sin City*, *Spy Kids*

☛ Darrell Hammond: Born October 8, 1955, in Melbourne; *Saturday Night Live*

☛ Victoria Jackson: Born August 2, 1959, in Miami; *Saturday Night Live*, *UHF*

☛ Catherine Keener: Born March 23, 1959, in Miami; *The 40-Year-Old Virgin*, *Being John Malkovich*

☛ William H. Macy: Born 1950 in Miami; *Boogie Nights*, *Seabiscuit*, *The Cooler*

☛ Butterfly McQueen: Born January 7, 1911, in Tampa; *Gone With the Wind*, *Beulah*

☛ Eva Mendes: Born March 5, 1974, in Miami; *Training Day*, *Hitch*, *Stuck on You*

☛ Moose (*Frasier*'s "Eddie"): Born December 24, 1990; died June 22, 2006

☞ Sarah Paulson: Born December 17, 1974, in Tampa; *Studio 60 on the Sunset Strip, Deadwood*

☞ Sir Sidney Poitier: Born February 20, 1927, in Miami; *The Defiant Ones, Guess Who's Coming to Dinner, To Sir, with Love*; first black actor to win an Oscar for a leading role for *Lilies of the Field*; appointed a Knight Commander of the Order of the British Empire

☞ Mimi Rogers: Born January 27, 1956, in Coral Gables; *Austin Powers, The Loop*

☞ Stephen Root: Born November 17, 1951, in Sarasota; *Office Space, NewsRadio*

☞ Wesley Snipes: Born July 31, 1962, in Orlando; *Blade, New Jack City, Jungle Fever*

☞ Wilmer Valderrama: Born January 30, 1980, in Miami; *That '70s Show, Fast Food Nation*

☞ Casper Van Dien: Born December 18, 1968, in Milton; *Starship Troopers, Sleepy Hollow*

☞ Ben Vereen: Born October 10, 1946, in Miami; *Roots, All That Jazz, Idlewild, Why Do Fools Fall in Love*

DID YOU KNOW?

Although he was criticized for portraying negative black stereotypes, the success of Stepin Fetchit (born Lincoln Theodore Perry on May 30, 1902, in Key West) opened the door for many future actors. In the course of his career, he acted in 54 films, was given a star on the Hollywood Walk of Fame and even won a Special Image Award from the NAACP.

The Dirt on Burt

Football hero, ladies' man, civic trailblazer, actor—it could only be Burt Reynolds! Reynolds has become a true Florida legend, which is all the more impressive considering he wasn't born in the state. Born in 1936 in Michigan, Burt grew up in Riviera Beach, where his father, a half-Cherokee, was the police chief. Burt went to Florida State University and made a name for himself as halfback on the Seminoles football team. He made the All-Southern Conference team, but a knee injury ended his sports career.

Burt turned to acting and soon became a regular in TV westerns such as *Gunsmoke*. His big break came when he starred in 1972's *Deliverance*, but he became a true movie star with such hit flicks as *The Longest Yard, Gator, Smokey and the Bandit* and the *Cannonball Run* series. This string of hits led to Burt being declared the number one box office star in the world. He also had a TV hit with the 1990–94 sitcom *Evening Shade*.

A long-time resident of Jupiter, Burt nurtured local actors and gave them roles at the Jupiter Theater, which he also founded. Reynolds also enjoyed a reputation as a ladies' man, romancing a wide array of Hollywood's hottest, including Sally Field, Dinah Shore (who was 19 years older) and especially his ex-wife, *WKRP in Cincinnati*'s Loni Anderson. Unfortunately, the couple's marriage ended with a highly publicized, bitter divorce. Reynolds' setbacks continued with his 1996 bankruptcy and the foreclosure of his theater. But he survived and even thrived, winning critical acclaim for his performance in *Boogie Nights*. Today, he's still in demand and now lives in Hobe Sound.

Reynolds Wraps

☛ According to the National Association of Theater Owners, Burt ranked among the top 10 box office stars in the world for 13 years, which had never before been accomplished.

☛ Reynolds has a star on the Hollywood Walk of Fame.

☛ In 1972, he posed semi-nude for *Playgirl* magazine. The issue, which was a huge seller, was the first American magazine to feature a (near) nude male.

☛ Reynolds was nominated for an Oscar; he has won a Golden Globe, an Emmy and 12 People's Choice awards.

☛ His college roommate was future ESPN football analyst and football coach Lee Corso.

Miami, the Center of Florida's Acting Universe

The Magic City has long enjoyed a reputation as a prime attraction for the film industry. On its 2006 list of America's movie-friendly cities, *MovieMaker Magazine* ranked Miami as number seven. The magazine consulted a variety of industry insiders, including writers, directors, location scouts and film commissioners. Over the last 40 years, Miami has played both leading and supporting roles in many movies and television shows.

Miami on the Big Screen

2 Fast 2 Furious (2003)
Ace Ventura: Pet Detective (1994)
Bad Boys (1995) and *Bad Boys II* (2003)
Scarface (1983)
The Birdcage (1996)
There's Something About Mary (1998)
True Lies (1994)

Miami on the Small Screen

CSI: Miami (2002–present)
Dave's World (1993–97)
The Golden Girls (1985–92)
Empty Nest (1988–95)
Nurses (1991–94)
The Jackie Gleason Show (1964–70)
Nip/Tuck (2003–present)
Surfside 6 (1960)

Films and TV Shows Filmed In and/or Set In the Sunshine State

Airport 77 (1976): Wakulla Springs
Basic (2003): Jacksonville
Caddyshack (1980): Boca Raton
Coach (TV show) (1989–97): Orlando
Cocoon (1985): St. Petersburg
Creature from the Black Lagoon (1954): Wakulla Springs
The Devil's Advocate (1997): Gainesville
Edward Scissorhands (1990): Tampa
Forces of Nature (1999): Jacksonville
G.I. Jane (1997): Jacksonville
I Dream of Jeannie (TV show) (1964–70): Cocoa Beach
Monster (2003): Sanford
My Girl (1991): Sanford

Paper Moon (1973): Boca Raton
The Real World: Miami (TV show) (1996): Miami
The Real World: Key West (TV show) (2006): Key West
Silk Stalkings (TV show) (1991–99): West Palm Beach
The Punisher (2004): Tampa
Why Do Fools Fall In Love (1998): Jacksonville

Vice Resident

And of course, there was a little show about two Miami cops that you may have heard of... From 1984 to 1990, one of the biggest hits on TV was *Miami Vice*, which had an enormously positive effect on the city's worldwide reputation, as well as on Don Johnson's career!

Besides pumping up tourism in Miami, the show inspired a flashy style and a moody feel for TV shows and music videos. It was also instrumental in determining men's fashions in the 1980s. And at its height, *Vice* attracted some of the music industry's biggest names, including U2, Phil Collins, the Police, Peter Gabriel, Bryan Adams, Tina Turner, Dire Straits, Depeche Mode and Billy Idol. The show was so popular that Jan Hammer's theme song reached number one on the *Billboard* charts.

As the legend goes, Brandon Tartikoff, who had been the head of NBC's Entertainment Division, had the idea for a show about "MTV cops." But while MTV's flashy videos definitely had an effect on the show, and vice versa, in reality, series creator Anthony Yerkovich said that the show was inspired by an article in *Time* magazine. The article dealt with a law stating that law enforcement agencies were able to use items recovered in the commission of a crime—such as sports cars, homes or jewelry—to further other unrelated investigations. Even after being canceled, *Miami Vice* remained a critical and fan favorite. The show's producer, Michael Mann, a noted film director, later returned to his popular characters; in 2006, the big screen *Vice* was released, starring Colin Farrell and Jamie Foxx.

DID YOU KNOW?

Throughout the 1950s and the 1960s, Miami was the site of one of the most influential production studios in the nation, Ivan Tors Studios. The studio worked on many family friendly hit TV shows, including *Sea Hunt* (1958–61), *Flipper* (1964–67) and *Gentle Ben* (1967–69).

The Cradle of Hispanic Programming

Being so close to Cuba, it's no surprise that Miami has become a destination for Hispanic television and film production. The city and its suburbs—especially Hialeah and Doral—are hailed for their Spanish-language television programming. Among the popular offerings are game shows, daytime talk shows, news programs and, of course, the addictive soap operas known as *telenovelas*. The first bilingual sitcom in the United States was produced, taped and aired in Miami. *¿Qué Pasa, USA?* ran from 1977 to 1979, airing on PBS affiliates nationwide.

Miami is also the home of Spanish-language variety shows, such as the most popular, *Sábado Gigante*, which is seen all over the world. These variety shows offer a diverse lineup of beautiful, scantily clad women, musicians, comedy, scantily clad women, interviews, scantily clad women and celebrities plugging their latest projects.

DID YOU KNOW?

Mega-popular video game *Grand Theft Auto: Vice City* is set in a fictional city inspired by Miami's architecture and geography. *Vice City* also features characters who speak Haitian Creole and Spanish, which boosts the Miami feel.

Jacksonville: Winter Film Capital of the World

Today, Miami dominates the state's entertainment scene. But in the early 1900s, another Florida city was hailed as the destination of choice for discriminating moviemakers everywhere. With its warm climate, exotic locations, newly perfected railway access and cheap labor, Jacksonville earned the title of the

"Winter Film Capital of the World" and attracted thousands of people from the film industry. From 1908 to 1920, when the majority of the studios relocated to California, Jacksonville was the site of more than 30 movie studios. And in that time, thousands of silent films were produced and released. Kalem Studio opened the city's first permanent studio in 1908, which lasted until 1917. In its history, it became the first studio to film year-round. Among Kalem's productions were the first cinematic releases of *Ben-Hur* and *Dr. Jeckyll and Mr. Hyde.* In the 1910s, Oliver Hardy—one-half of one of the world's most famous comedy duos, Laurel and Hardy—made his first movies in Jacksonville.

Televised Tragedy

On July 15, 1974, a Sarasota TV reporter shocked viewers when she committed suicide during a live television broadcast. Christine Chubbuck, the hostess of the WXLT's community affairs talk show, *Suncoast Digest*, had been plagued by depression and thoughts of suicide. Contributing to her deteriorating state of mind was her lack of a social life and an unrequited crush on a colleague. And to make matters worse, Chubbuck's mother allegedly knew of her daughter's mental situation and chose not to inform her employers, fearing that Christine would be fired as a result.

According to reports, Chubbuck received the approval to do a piece about suicide, and then consulted with police about methods of suicide. She was told that one of the most effective methods was using a .38-caliber revolver with wad-cutter target bullets to shoot oneself in the back of the head, as opposed to the temple. Chubbuck even joked with her colleagues about killing herself on air, and she allegedly inserted a story about her impending suicide in her news copy.

Once the cameras were rolling, Chubbuck pulled out a revolver and shot herself behind her right ear. She fell forward and the screen faded to black. The news crew thought it was a prank until Chubbuck's body began twitching. She was rushed to the hospital and was pronounced dead 14 hours later. An estimated 120 people attended Chubbuck's funeral, and all three national TV networks reported her death. However, the networks' hopes of a juicier story were dashed when the family got an injunction against the station, preventing the release of the suicide video.

The Rise and Fall of Pee-Wee Herman

By the early 1990s, Paul "Pee-Wee Herman" Reubens was a certified superstar, popular with both kids and their parents. But his rising star imploded in a big way, and of course, it happened in Florida. In the blink of an eye, "Pee-Wee" was no more!

On July 26, 1991, county sheriffs arrested Reubens for lewd conduct (masturbating publicly) in a Sarasota adult movie theater. Naturally, the news media jumped on the story, and quickly, both the actor and his beloved alter ego were reduced to a punch line. The TV series *Pee-Wee's Playhouse* had been canceled by that time, but CBS dropped the reruns from its schedule. Legally, Reubens made out okay. He made a deal with the Sarasota County court and received a fine and made a few public service announcements in exchange for a clean record.

On September 5, 1991, Reubens made a surprise appearance—as Pee-Wee—at the MTV Video Music Awards. Showing he could still take a joke, Pee-Wee received a standing ovation when he asked the audience, "Heard any good jokes lately?" Proving that audiences can forgive anything, Pee-Wee is making a comeback and has even been working on a new movie!

INVENTIONS, DISCOVERIES AND TECHNOLOGIES, OH MY!

Plane Truths

It's only fitting that a state that welcomes so many airline passengers should be the birthplace of commercial aviation! On New Year's Day in 1914, the world's first scheduled commercial airline service "took flight" with the St. Petersburg–Tampa Airboat Line, which flew two daily round trips for 28 consecutive days. The infant airline had one airplane, a Benoist "flying boat," which had a capacity of one pilot and one passenger, as well as room for a little cargo. The flight's pilot later became the namesake of the Tampa Chamber of Commerce's Tony Jannus Award, which was presented annually for achievement in commercial aviation. On the airline's maiden voyage, the passenger was A.C. Pheil, a former mayor St. Petersburg.

Gainesville, the Birthplace of Gatorade

Back in the 1960s, we were living in the Dark Ages when it came to exercising and working out. Fortunately, some brilliant thinkers at the University of Florida (UF), home of the Gators, decided to do some much-needed research. With its brutal heat and humidity, Florida proved to be the perfect testing ground for such research.

So, in early summer 1965, a UF assistant football coach, along with a team of university physicians, began exploring the reasons why so many of the school's players were being affected by heat and heat-related illnesses. They discovered that there were two key factors at work.

1. The players were losing precious fluids and electrolytes through sweat that were not being replaced; and

2. The players were using large amounts of carbohydrates for energy that were not being replenished.

Adjourning to the laboratory, the research team soon formulated a precisely balanced carbohydrate and electrolyte beverage designed to replenish the key components lost through sweat and exercise. Because the researchers were helping the Gators, they named their miracle drink Gatorade. And once the researchers introduced the drink to the Gator football team, the players coincidentally began winning games. The Gators ended the season with a 7–4 record—their first winning season in more than a decade. The next season, they earned a 9–2 record and won the Orange Bowl for the first time in the school's history!

The secret of Gatorade leaked out, and soon other college football programs across the country ordered the drink. In 1969, Gatorade was chosen as the NFL's official sports drink, a title it holds to this day. And today, Gatorade, long the market leader for thirst quenching, is found on the sidelines of virtually every school and professional team in the nation. It has resulted in more than $80 million for UF, which has been used to fund a variety of school programs. Gatorade's slogan asks, "Is it in you?" And for almost every athlete, exerciser or thirsty man or woman, the answer is probably "yes!"

"Lawn" Live the Snappin' Turtle!

In 1933, Montverde resident Neil Smith and his brother developed the first Snapper riding lawn mower. Known as the Snappin' Turtle, the heavy, bright green mower sported a shiny turtle head ornament on its hood. The Snappin' Turtle was self-controlled and could cut grass, bushes and small trees. The Snapper Corporation still uses the original machine's patent to this day.

"Here Comes the Sun" (Screen)

With World War II in full swing, soldiers were dealing with severe sunburns on top of their many other problems. A solution was needed, and Benjamin Green, a Miami Beach pharmacist, came to the rescue.

In 1944, he cooked cocoa butter in a granite coffee pot on his wife's stove and created a sticky, red substance that he called "red vet pet" (red veterinary petrolatum). Green tested the thick, petroleum-based, Vaseline-like concoction on his own bald head and found that the cream effectively blocked the sun's rays. And thus was born one truly sweet-smelling sunblock, as well as a great boon for state tourism!

No stranger to outdoor sports enthusiasts, Miami is the home of the first automated teller bank machine (ATM) designed specifically for rollerbladers.

Bridging the Gap

Tampa is home to the Sunshine Skyway Bridge, a cable-stayed concrete bridge soaring to heights of 190 feet above the water. Opened in 1987, the bridge sports bright yellow support cables spreading out from the two center pillars. The views from the bridge are visually striking; drivers have an unobstructed view of the water during the 5.5-mile trip over Tampa Bay.

Spanning the St. Johns River northeast of downtown Jacksonville, the Dames Point Bridge is more than two miles long. And while the Sunshine Skyway Bridge is the world's longest cable-stayed concrete bridge, the Dames Point Bridge ranks as the longest cable-stayed span bridge in the Western Hemisphere. Completed in 1989, the bridge rises 175 feet above the main channel of the river.

DID YOU KNOW?

The world's largest telescope, scheduled to be unveiled in 2007 in the Canary Islands, is being constructed through a partnership between Spain and the University of Florida.

Thomas Edison's Florida Paradise

As he got older, Thomas Alva Edison fell in love with the warm weather of Florida, and in the 1880s, the inventor bought land in Fort Myers, which at the time had 349 people. Edison had been spending winters in Fort Myers, with his first wife, Mary, who died in 1884. With his second wife, Mina, at his side,

Edison spent more and more time in Fort Myers and built his home away from home, Seminole Lodge.

Although he'd already had great success with his inventions, such as the electric light and the phonograph, he didn't rest on his laurels. In the small laboratory of Seminole Lodge, Edison continued to work on projects, including using bamboo fiber as an electric light filament, searching for a rubber-producing domestic plant and even contributing to automobile technology. Edison built one of the first cement-lined swimming pools in Florida, using a nearby artesian well to both fill the pool and irrigate the botanical gardens.

Edison also helped Fort Myers achieve respect as it grew into a city, and he even imported 2000 royal palms from Cuba to plant along the city's main thoroughfares. Today, a local community college bears his name, and in 1937, six years after his death, Fort Myers began celebrating the Pageant of Light every February to honor Edison's life and legacy.

Ice Ice Baby!

Raise an icy drink to the memory of Dr. John Gorrie, the "Ice Man" of Florida. In the 1830s, the state, especially the Gulf Coast, was in the grip of a cholera epidemic and a yellow fever epidemic. Yellow fever was particularly heinous; not only was there no cure, but as many as 70 percent of all who were afflicted died, and in as quickly as 10 hours! The symptoms included chills, fever, thirst, backaches, jaundice and vomiting of blood. Any solution was sought out and tried. And one of the most effective treatments proved to be cooling patients' rooms.

Gorrie, an Apalachicola physician, wanted to help his neighbors, and he knew that the cooling method had great potential. In 1842, Gorrie experimented with compressor technology at his Apalachicola hospital and created ice, which he then used to cool the air for his patients. Gorrie envisioned using his ice-making machine to regulate the temperature of entire buildings, and eventually, entire cities. Gorrie's ice-making machine was awarded a patent in 1851. Unfortunately, his chief financial backer died, and Gorrie was unable to get the necessary funding to develop the machine. He died in poverty in 1855, and we would have to wait another 50 years for air conditioning to be invented. Nevertheless, the world, and Florida especially, owes a huge debt of gratitude to Dr. John Gorrie, the father of refrigeration and air conditioning!

Concentrated Goodness

You may have never heard their names: Louis Gardner MacDowell of Lakeland, Cedric Donald Atkins of Winter Haven and Edwin L. Moore of Lake Alfred. But it's a safe bet that you've enjoyed a big glass of their hard work!

In 1942, these three men, all employees of the Florida Citrus Commission, were given the task of creating a new orange juice product that could be easily transported to troops stuck on European battlefields. Together, MacDowell, Atkins and Moore developed concentrated orange juice. For three years, the team worked in Winter Haven to develop the product, as well as a cost-effective way to make it. They finally perfected the method; it involved evaporating the water from the orange juice at 80°F, and then returning a small, tasty amount of fresh juice. They then chilled, canned and froze the solution.

The concentrated solution was awarded a patent on November 9, 1948, which was claimed by the U.S. Department of Agriculture. The orange juice concentrate revolutionized Florida's citrus industry. The state quickly became the leading orange juice producer in the nation, and even made orange juice the official drink of Florida. And what of the inventors? As a reward for their efforts, the three men, all good civil servants, were given six months of vacation time—even though no more than six weeks could be used in any single year!

DID YOU **KNOW?**

Alienware Corporation, one of the computer industry's shining stars, was founded in Miami in 1996. The company is highly regarded for its state-of-the-art computer laptop and desktop technologies, especially for audio/video editing and gaming. Alienware, named after the founders' great love for the *X-Files*, is now a wholly owned subsidiary of the Dell Computer Corporation.

LAW AND ORDER IS A LITTLE DIFFERENT IN FLORIDA

Living in Paradise?

Every year, the U.S. government ranks the most dangerous cities and states. And according to the 2006 rankings, Florida came in at number seven (although this was down from number six in 2005). Meanwhile, three Florida cities—Tampa, West Palm Beach and Miami—and four metropolitan areas—Miami, Tallahassee, Gainesville and Tampa-St. Petersburg-Clearwater—rank among the most dangerous in the United States. The FBI concurs, as it ranks the Miami metro area as the second worst nationwide, based on the number of murders, rapes, robberies, aggravated assaults, burglaries and motor vehicle thefts that have occurred there.

But there is a tiny flicker of good news, crime-wise! From 2004 to 2005, Florida did experience a decrease in the number and rate of total crime, as well as property crimes. And although violent crimes increased slightly, the rate per 100,000 people did go down. Here are the numbers for 2005:

Total Violent Crimes: 125,825

Murders: 881
Forcible Sex Offenses: 12,230
Robberies: 30,092
Aggravated Assaults: 82,622
(Percent change from 2004: 1.7 percent)

Violent crime rate per 100,000 people: 702.2
(Percent change from 2004: –0.6 percent)

Total Property Crimes: 712,238

Burglaries: 164,777
Larcenies: 472,257
Motor Vehicle Thefts: 75,204
(Percent change from 2004: –2.0 percent)

Property crime rate per 100,000 people: 3974.9
(Percent change from 2004: –4.2 percent)

2005 Total Index Crime: 838,063

DID YOU  KNOW?

According to research, Florida ranks third nationwide in the number of death row inmates, after California and Texas. The state is also third in number of executions since 1976, after Texas and Virginia. From 1976 to October 2000, Florida executed 49 inmates.

Mortgaging Your Future

Here's a not-so-flattering achievement: Florida leads the nation in mortgage fraud. According to Fannie Mae, a leading financial services company serving the American home mortgage industry, in September 2006, Florida reported the highest rates of misrepresentations on mortgage applications over the past year. To make matters worse, Florida now leads in complaints of suspect activity filed by banks and other lenders. And when it comes to the amount of loans defaulting early, Florida comes in second, after New Orleans.

Police State

Miami is the home of the American Police Hall of Fame and Museum (APHF). Founded in 1960, this museum is the first national police museum and memorial dedicated to American law enforcement officers killed in the line of duty. The goal of the APHF is to educate the public about American law enforcement's history and the current trends. Visitors to the museum are treated to interactive displays, simulators and nearly 11,000 artifacts. Every year on May 15, which is Police Memorial Day, the APHF invites hundreds of police officers, as well as their families and friends, and dignitaries to an event that celebrates the hard work of these brave men and women. The day is also a painful reminder that in the United States, a police officer is killed in the line of duty every 57 hours.

FLORIDA'S LOOPIEST LAWS

Statewide Laws

☛ Livestock cannot be put on a school bus.

☛ Women falling asleep under a hair dryer risk a fine, as do the salon owners.

☛ Pregnant pigs must not be confined in cages.

☛ All doors of public buildings must open outward.

☛ It is illegal to sell your children.

☛ Unmarried women must not parachute on Sunday, risking a fine, arrest and/or jail.

☛ When tying an elephant to a parking meter, the parking fee must be paid as for any other vehicle.

☛ Singing in public places while wearing a swimsuit is illegal.

☛ Men are forbidden from being seen publicly in any strapless gown.

☛ Skateboarding without a license is against the law.

☛ Absolutely no passing gas in public places after 6:00 PM.

☛ Horse theft is punishable by hanging.

☛ Topless walking or running within a 150-foot zone between the beach and the street is prohibited.

City and County Laws

Big Pine Key: Molesting Key deer is illegal.

Broward County: People working at hot dog stands may not be "inappropriately attired."

Cape Coral:

☛ Clothes can't be hung outside on clotheslines.

☛ Pick-up trucks must not be parked in driveways or in front of houses on the street.

☛ If you leave a couch to sit in your driveway, you risk a $50 fine.

Daytona Beach:

☛ It is illegal to molest trash cans.

☛ It's a public nuisance to own a water-filled flower pot incapable of draining.

Destin:

☛ Storeowners may not permit people to distribute free ducklings in front of the store.

☛ You must get dressed in your hotel room if you plan to swim in the ocean.

☛ Torpedoes may not be set off within the city.

☛ You may not lean a bicycle against a tree in a cemetery; you may not drive over graves in a cemetery; it is illegal to sell ice cream in a cemetery.

Hialeah: Ambling and strolling is a misdemeanor.

Jacksonville: Molesting squirrels is a Class A misdemeanor.

Key West: Chickens are considered a protected species.

Miami-Dade County:
- ☛ This is the only county in which it is illegal to sell, purchase, obtain, keep, maintain or harbor pit bulls, or even to bring them into the county.

- ☛ Imitating animals is prohibited.

Miami Beach:
- ☛ Skateboarding is not allowed at police stations.

- ☛ Persons selling oranges on the sidewalk face up to 30 days in jail.

- ☛ Termite farms are prohibited within the city.

- ☛ Pigs are banned from all beaches.

Naples: Neon signs are prohibited.

Palm Bay: Persons on bicycles may not tow sleds.

Pensacola:
- ☛ Citizens may not go downtown without having at least $10 on their person.

- ☛ Rolling barrels on any street is illegal; fines vary depending on the contents.

- ☛ Women killed by electrocution in bathtubs can be fined (only after death).

Pinecrest: Permits are required to operate burglar alarms.

Sanford: Stage nudity is banned, unless at "bona fide" theatrical performances.

Sarasota:

☛ If you hit a pedestrian, you'll be fined $78.

☛ Catching crabs is prohibited.

Satellite Beach: It's illegal for people to appear in public wearing liquid latex.

Tampa:

☛ Topless dancers are forbidden to expose their breasts while performing.

☛ Lap dancers must stay six feet away from customers.

West Palm Beach: At one time, the roofs of all outhouses were required to be fireproof.

If You're Gonna Do the Crime...

Jill Knispel, 35, stole a rare greenwing parrot worth $2000 from a Fort Myers exotic bird store by hiding the bird in her bra. But when she went to trade the parrot for a vintage car, she made the mistake of gossiping to the car's owner about how she had acquired her feathered friend. It just so happened that the car owner was buddies with the bird's owner. And bird-brained Knispel was charged with grand theft.

After being arrested in Tampa for drunk driving, Paul Domenech, 34, was found innocent by the jury. His defense? A professional fire-breather, Domenech claimed that the alcohol that officers smelled on his breath was actually a mixture of rubbing alcohol and gasoline that he had just used for work.

Wayne Lewis, 24, a 475-pound Miami resident, was arrested at the Tallahassee airport for possession of cocaine. He had been identified by drug-sniffing dogs, but when police were unable to find any contraband, they began to suspect the dogs' sniffing abilities. However, it turned out that the drugs did exist; Lewis had hidden almost 11 pounds of crack cocaine in the folds of his mighty stomach!

In 1998, Paul Shimkonis of Pinellas County went to see one of his favorite performers, Tawny Peaks (Michele Ann Laird), at Diamond Dolls nightclub in Clearwater. After a particularly energetic dance, Shimkonis sued Peaks, claiming that she had caused him whiplash by swinging her massive mammaries into his face. Shimkonis claimed that the breasts were as hard as cement blocks. The case ended up on the *People's Court*, where Judge Ed Koch ruled in favor of Peaks. The stripper later retired from modeling and stripping and is now a Michigan housewife. In 2005, she sold her breast implants on eBay for more than $16,000!

Master illusionist David Copperfield put his talents to good use—he prevented a robbery against himself! In April 2006, Copperfield and his two female assistants were robbed at gunpoint by four teenagers in West Palm Beach following a performance. Although his assistants handed over money, passports and a cell phone, Copperfield reportedly used sleight of hand to hide his possessions. One of his assistants wrote down most of the license plate number of the getaway car, and the suspects were arrested.

World-famous tennis star Anna Kournikova was searching for a different type of court when a homeless man was accused of swimming nude across Biscayne Bay in search of her Miami waterfront home. William Lepeska, 40, was apprehended in the swimming pool of Kournikova's next-door neighbor's home. According to police, as Lepeska was taken away, he was screaming "Anna! Save me!"

NOTORIOUS CRIMINALS

Giuseppe Zangara

On February 15, 1933, this Italian immigrant attended a speech being given by President-elect Franklin Delano Roosevelt (FDR) at Miami's Bayfront Park. Zangara, a local resident, concealed a .32-caliber pistol, with the intention of killing FDR. But at only five feet tall, he was unable to get a clear shot. Zangara managed to shoot six times before he was stopped, and though FDR wasn't hit, five others were, including Chicago's mayor, Anton Cermak, who had been sitting next to Roosevelt. Cermak, the only casualty, died two days after Roosevelt's inauguration. On March 20, 1933, Zangara was executed in "Old Sparky," the state's electric chair, shortly after being convicted of Cermak's murder.

There was speculation that Zangara, a poorly educated brick-layer, had been driven insane by constant sharp pain from his gallbladder. Unable to work, he came to believe that his pain was being caused by then-president Herbert Hoover. But other sources believe that Zangara may have been driven to attempted murder by loneliness, as well as by envy for those in power. What was clear was that Zangara had no real hatred towards either Hoover or Roosevelt; he was even heard to say, "Hoover and Roosevelt—everybody the same."

Al Capone

Although considered by many to be the greatest gang leader in history, Capone was welcomed with open arms in many cities. Miami Beach, though, was not on that list. In 1928, Capone, a new resident of Miami Beach, made many attempts to fit in but with little success. The city, which had been trying to survive a slowdown in the land boom, as well as 1926's devastating hurricane, didn't need new reasons for tourists to stay away!

The governor ordered sheriffs to arrest Capone on sight. However, multiple arrests and constant surveillance couldn't slow down Capone, who continued planning his 1929 Valentine's Day Massacre in Chicago. Although the execution-style murder was never officially pinned on Capone, it did make authorities more eager than ever to take him down for good. In 1930, Capone was named Public Enemy Number One, and a year later, he was convicted of tax evasion, sentenced to 11 years in prison and fined tens of thousands of dollars. He was transferred to Alcatraz in 1934, but as he had contracted syphilis, Capone's sentence was shortened to six and a half years. On January 25, 1947, he died of cardiac arrest.

Aileen Wuornos

The subject of the Oscar-winning 2003 movie *Monster*, this prostitute (actually a Michigan native) killed seven men in Florida. In each case, the meeting began as ordinary sex, but when Wuornos felt that the man was becoming abusive, she would repeatedly shoot her victim in the chest or in the back of the head with a .22-caliber handgun, rob him and hide the body in the woods. Among her victims were police officers, a missionary, a known rapist and truck drivers. After the police tracked down Wuornos, she confessed to all seven murders but claimed self-defense for all of them. At her 1992 trial, any credibility Wuornos had was destroyed when her lesbian lover (who had never participated in the murders) testified against her. Her self-defense claim was thrown out, and the jury felt no sympathy. Sentenced to the electric chair, Wuornos was executed by lethal injection on October 9, 2002.

Martha Beck and Raymond Fernandez

Better known as the "Lonely Hearts Killers," this couple from Pensacola murdered 20 women throughout the country. Posing as brother and sister, the deadly duo placed misleading personal ads to attract female victims to companionship or matrimony. The prize for these unwilling targets was Raymond himself, as women were attracted to this Hawaiian-Latino heartthrob. And if the victims resisted or caught on to the personal ad scam, the couple beat them to death. Martha would also slip into a jealous rage and kill when she felt that Raymond and a victim were getting too close. On August 18, 1949, a jury found Fernandez and Beck guilty of first-degree murder, and they were sent to Sing-Sing. The couple was executed by electric chair on March 8, 1951.

Christine Falling

Between 1980 and 1982, this teenaged babysitter from Perry murdered at least five neighborhood children by suffocation. She claimed that voices commanded her to do it to prevent anyone from hearing the screaming. Falling, who was considered "dim-witted," was sentenced to three concurrent life sentences and imprisoned. In 2007, she will have her first opportunity to apply for parole.

Ted Bundy

Considered one of the most notorious murderers in U.S. history, Theodore Robert Bundy eventually confessed to killing more than 30 women. However, the total number may never be known. Bundy was diagnosed as a sociopath, and like most serial killers, he was described as being educated, handsome and charming, despite his brutal crimes. While in prison, Bundy received about 200 fan letters every day from female admirers. On January 24, 1989, at the age of 42, Bundy was executed in "Old Sparky."

Danny Rolling

Also known as the "Gainesville Ripper," Rolling ultimately confessed to killing eight people. In August 1990, Rolling threw Gainesville into a state of panic after the bodies of five young students were discovered in their apartments. Rolling eventually confessed to these killings, and to raping several of his victims. He also confessed to a 1989 triple homicide in Shreveport, Louisiana, and admitted attempting to murder his father in May 1990. On October 25, 2006, Rolling was executed by lethal injection after the U.S. Supreme Court rejected his last-ditch appeal.

A Starke Reminder

Florida State Prison (FSP), also known as Starke Prison (it is located near the town of Starke) or Raiford Prison, is a maximum-security facility. Here are some arresting details:

- ☛ FSP is one of the state's largest prisons, housing over 1400 of the most dangerous inmates.

- ☛ It is the state's only prison, as the other institutions are called correctional facilities.

- ☛ FSP is a totally indoor institution; no inmate ever has to leave the indoor facility.

- ☛ The institution opened in 1961, even though construction was not completed until 1968.

- ☛ FSP houses the state's death row and execution chamber.

- ☛ (In)famous former inmates include Ted Bundy, Danny Rolling and Aileen Wuornos.

- ☛ Lynyrd Skynyrd's song "Four Walls of Raiford" is about a convict escaping from the prison.

The Murder of Gianni Versace

Throughout the 1980s and 1990s, Giovanni "Gianni" Versace was the undisputed king of fashion, and his designs were the toast of Broadway and Hollywood alike. But on July 15, 1997, Versace was gunned down in front of his Miami Beach oceanfront mansion. The police reported that Versace had been murdered by spree killer Andrew Cunanan, who committed suicide shortly after the murder using the same handgun. After shooting Versace, Cunanan fled to a Miami houseboat (which he was thought to be living on) to avoid being captured, and on July 23, he committed suicide. There was speculation that killing Versace may have had something to do with Cunanan's possible HIV diagnosis. Cunanan was thought to engage in prostitution with older men, and indeed, most of his victims fit that description.

Versace, born in Reggio Calabria, Italy, on December 2, 1946, had amassed a fashion empire worth $808 million. The designer was a favorite of supermodels, celebrities, musicians and even royalty such as Princess Diana and Princess Caroline. Later, the designer made clothes for the theater and television communities. In fact, it was his hiring as costume designer for *Miami Vice* that led to Versace's move to Miami Beach. After being diagnosed with a rare cancer of the inner ear, Versace was said to be in remission, and he made it a habit to take regular walks on Miami Beach's world-famous Ocean Drive until his untimely death.

In September 1997, Versace's brother Santo was announced as the company's new CEO, while his sister Donatella was selected as the new head of design. Elton John's 1997 album, *The Big Picture*, was dedicated to Versace.

THE SPORTING LIFE

The University of Florida's Twin Triumphs

The University of Florida had already achieved incredible success with the creation of Gatorade. But the athletic department would experience its greatest victories in the 1990s and into the new millennium. First, the football team, under the leadership of Coach Steve Spurrier, a former Gator himself, won the 1996 National Championship in the Sugar Bowl. But that was just a tasty appetizer, compared to the Gators' 2006 scorecard. The team accomplished two incredibly rare and impressive achievements. First, the men's basketball team won the school's first ever men's basketball championship. Then, the football team won the football national championship for the second time. This was the first time a university or college had ever won two championships in one year!

DID YOU KNOW?

With so many colleges and such beautiful year-round weather, it's no wonder that Florida hosts more college football games than any other state.

Sports Stars from the Sunshine State

☞ Isaac Bruce: Born November 10, 1972, in Fort Lauderdale; wide receiver for the Los Angeles Rams.

☞ Steven "Lefty" Carlton: Born December 22, 1944, in Miami; considered one of the most successful pitchers ever, Carlton played for various teams, including the St. Louis Cardinals, Philadelphia Phillies, Chicago White Sox, San Francisco Giants, Cleveland Indians and Minnesota Twins.

☞ Laveranues Coles: Born December 29, 1977, in Jacksonville; wide receiver for the New York Jets (and briefly the

Washington Redskins). Considered one of football's fastest players, Coles played wide receiver for Florida State University. Unfortunately, in October 1999, Coles and another player, wide receiver Peter Warrick, conspired with a cashier at a local department store to steal over $400 worth of clothes and shoes, while paying only $21.40. They were charged with felony grand theft, and Coles was dismissed from the team.

☛ Andre "the Hawk" Dawson: Born July 10, 1954, in Miami; former Montreal Expos outfielder.

☛ David Duval: Born November 9, 1971, in Jacksonville; professional golfer and winner of the President's Cup. From 1997 to 2001, he won 13 PGA tournaments, including the Tour Championship in 1997, the 1999 Players Championship, the 2000 World Cup (with Tiger Woods) and the 2001 Dunlop Phoenix Open. Duval ranked number one in the Official World Golf Rankings in April 1999.

☛ Chris Evert: Born December 21, 1954, in Fort Lauderdale; formerly ranked No. 1 in the world in women's tennis. Evert's career win-loss record in singles matches of 1309–146 (.900) is the best of any professional player in tennis history! She won 18 Grand Slam singles titles, including a record seven at the French Open. She also won three Grand Slam doubles titles. By and large, Evert is considered one of the greatest female tennis players of all time.

☛ Dwight "Doc," "Dr. K" Gooden: Born November 16, 1964, in Tampa; pitcher for the New York Mets, New York Yankees, Cleveland Indians, Houston Astros and Tampa Bay Devil Rays. His awards include Rookie of the Year (NL) 1984; Cy Young Award (NL) 1985; and Sporting News Player of the Year (NL) 1985. He is the N.Y. Mets career leader in win-loss average (.649).

☛ Brian Griese: Born March 18, 1975, in Miami; quarterback for the Chicago Bears. Griese is the son of legendary Miami Dolphins quarterback Bob Griese.

- Michael "the Play Maker" Irvin: Born March 5, 1966, in Fort Lauderdale; Dallas Cowboys wide receiver. He is regarded as one of the NFL's most successful wide receivers ever; in February of 2007, he was inducted into the Pro Football Hall of Fame.

- Chad Johnson: Born January 9, 1978, in Miami; wide receiver for the Cincinnati Bengals.

- Roy Jones Jr.: Born January 16, 1969, in Pensacola; former Middleweight, Super Middleweight, Light Heavyweight and Heavyweight boxing champion of the world. Jones was *Ring Magazine*'s "Fighter of the Year" in 1994, and the Boxing Writers of America voted him "Fighter of the Decade" in 1999. Many experts considered Jones the best pound-for-pound fighter in the world from 1999 to 2003.

- Jevon "the Freak" Kearse: Born September 3, 1976, in Fort Myers; defensive end for the Philadelphia Eagles. He got his nickname from his combination of athleticism and threatening style of play.

- Shaun King: Born May 29, 1977, in St. Petersburg; quarterback for the Tampa Bay Buccaneers, his hometown team. King carried the team to a victory over the Washington Redskins in the 1999 divisional playoffs. A week later, the Bucs fell just short of playing in Super Bowl XXXIV, losing 11–6 to the St. Louis Rams in the NFC Championship game.

- Willis McGahee: Born October 20, 1981, in Miami; running back for the Buffalo Bills.

- Rena "Sable" Mero: Born August 8, 1967, in Jacksonville; Mero has carved out a career as a professional wrestler, model and actress. As one of the original WWE Divas, she broke hearts (and bones) in the World Wrestling Entertainment (WWE) league. In April 1999, Sable posed for *Playboy*. She has left and returned to wrestling repeatedly over the years.

☛ Andrew Miller: Born May 21, 1985, in Gainesville; pitcher for the Detroit Tigers.

☛ Santana Moss: Born June 1, 1979, in Miami; wide receiver for the Washington Redskins.

☛ Rodney Mullen: Born August 17, 1966, in Gainesville; widely considered one of history's most influential skateboarders. Mullen is revered for creating virtually every street and vertical skateboarding flip trick used in the 1980s and early 1990s. Among his inventions are the kickflip, the heelflip, the 360 flip, the flat-ground ollie and the Impossible.

☛ Emmitt Smith: Born May 15, 1969, in Pensacola; running back for the Dallas Cowboys and Arizona Cardinals. This former UF Gator, a three-time Super Bowl champion, is the NFL's all-time rushing leader—a record previously held by his hero, Walter Payton. He is the only running back to ever have won a Super Bowl, the NFL Most Valuable Player (MVP) Award and the NFL rushing crown all in one (1993) season! Smith retired in 2005 and became a studio analyst on *NFL Total Access*. On July 21, 2007, Smith was inducted into the College Football Hall of Fame. Oh, in the fall of 2006, you may have seen Smith strut his stuff on ABC's *Dancing with the Stars*. Smith wowed the judges and the audience and was declared the winner. Take that, Jerry Springer!

☛ Steve Spurrier: Born April 20, 1945, in Miami Beach; two-time All-American and member of the College Football Hall of Fame. Spurrier won the Heisman Trophy in 1966. As coach for the University of Florida football team, he took them to six SEC championships from 1991 to 2000 and won the 1996 National Championship. Today, Spurrier is the coach for the University of South Carolina Gamecocks.

☞ Danny Wuerffel: Born May 27, 1974, in Pensacola; former quarterback for the University of Florida. He won the 1996 Heisman Trophy while playing under coach Steve Spurrier and went on to play for various professionla teams, including the New Orleans Saints, Green Bay Packers, Chicago Bears and Washington Redskins.

☞ Jack Youngblood: Born January 26, 1950, in Jacksonville; a former Gator, Youngblood went on to play defensive end for the Los Angeles Rams.

☞ On September 30, 2006, Jack Youngblood and fellow Gators Steve Spurrier, Danny Wuerffel and Emmitt Smith were inducted into the Florida Football Ring of Honor.

Deion Sanders: Two Sports, One Superstar

Deion Sanders ("Neon Deion," "Prime Time") was born on August 9, 1967, in Fort Myers. A triple threat for the Florida State University Seminoles, Sanders played on the football, base-ball and track and field teams. Professionally, Sanders excelled in both the National Football League and Major League Baseball. Considered one of the best cornerbacks ever, Sanders played for the Atlanta Falcons, San Francisco 49ers, Dallas Cowboys, Washington Redskins and Baltimore Ravens. As a baseball player, Sanders played outfield for the New York Yankees, Atlanta Braves, Cincinnati Reds and San Francisco Giants. Today, he works for the NFL Network as an on-air analyst. Here are some "Prime Time" ratings:

☞ In 1989, Sanders hit a home run in MLB and scored a touchdown in the NFL in the same week, something never before accomplished.

☞ At FSU, Sanders played the first game of a baseball double-header, ran a leg of a 4x100 relay and returned to play another baseball game—all in one day!

- Under FSU football coach Bobby Bowden, Sanders was a two-time All-American cornerback (1987, 1988) and a third team All-American (1986).

- He intercepted 14 passes in his college career.

- Sanders won the Jim Thorpe Award in 1988.

- In 1988, he led the nation with his punt return average, breaking the FSU record for career punt return yards.

- His FSU jersey, number 2, was retired in 1995.

What Happens in Tampa, Stays in Tampa!

In November 2005, police busted a 40-foot motor home that had been converted into a strip club—complete with alcohol and lap dances—parked outside Raymond James Stadium for Tampa Bay Buccaneers games. According to reports, the women inside the motor home had been charging a $20 cover, plus $20 to $40 depending on whether the customers wanted topless or totally nude dancing. In addition, people had been caught smoking marijuana in the mobile home, which was there to advertise a nearby strip club.

Amazingly, that's not the only Tampa/football/sex story that occurred in November 2005! Police were called to break up two Carolina Panthers cheerleaders caught brawling in the bathroom of Banana Joes' nightclub. There were also allegations that the two cheerleaders, who were inevitably fired, were having sex with each other, though the women denied the claim.

Dolphins Details

- In 1966, the Miami Dolphins became Florida's first permanent, major league–level professional sports team.

- The Dolphins joined the American Football League (AFL) in 1965 as an expansion team franchise bought for $7.5 million by Joseph Robbie, a lawyer, and actor Danny Thomas.

☛ The team name was the winning entry in a 1965 contest for which almost 20,000 entries were submitted. According to Robbie, the name "Dolphins" was picked because dolphins are one of the fastest and smartest creatures of the sea. "Dolphins can attack and kill a shark or a whale. Sailors say bad luck will come to anyone who harms one of them."

☛ Don Shula coached the team from the very beginning until 1995. Shula, the winningest head coach in professional football history, led the Dolphins to 24 out of 26 winning seasons.

☛ During the 1972 season, the Dolphins became the first and only NFL team to win a 14-game regular season, the entire postseason and the Super Bowl (Super Bowl VII)!

☛ The next season, the team won Super Bowl VIII, becoming the first team to appear in three consecutive Super Bowls. The Dolphins were also the second overall team, and the first AFL/AFC team, to win back-to-back championships.

☛ During the 1970s, six future Hall of Fame members played for Miami, including quarterback Bob Griese and running back Larry Csonka.

☛ Throughout the 1980s and 1990s, quarterback Dan Marino became the NFL's most prolific passer ever!

DID YOU KNOW?

Way before the Miami Heat became the 2006 NBA National Champions, the Miami Floridians were the state's resident basketball franchise. The Floridians played for the now-defunct American Basketball Association (ABA) from 1968 to 1972. Sporting two different color schemes—the original red, blue and white, and then black, magenta and orange—the team made it to the playoffs in three out of four of their seasons.

Your Guide to the Grapefruit League

When the weather cools off in the rest of the country, professional baseball teams look to the warmth of Central and South Florida. Almost two-thirds of all MLB teams spend spring training at Floridian locations. Here's the rundown:

☞ Atlanta Braves: Cracker Jack Stadium, Lake Buena Vista

☞ Baltimore Orioles: Fort Lauderdale Stadium, Fort Lauderdale

☞ Boston Red Sox: City of Palms Park, Fort Myers

☞ Cincinnati Reds: Ed Smith Stadium, Sarasota

☞ Cleveland Indians: Chain of Lakes Park, Winter Haven

☞ Detroit Tigers: Joker Marchant Stadium, Lakeland

☞ Florida Marlins: Roger Dean Stadium, Jupiter

☞ Houston Astros: Osceola County Stadium, Kissimmee

☞ Los Angeles Dodgers: Holman Stadium, Vero Beach

☞ Minnesota Twins: Hammond Stadium, Fort Myers

☞ New York Mets: Tradition Field, Port St. Lucie

☞ New York Yankees: Legends Field, Tampa

☞ Philadelphia Phillies: Bright House Networks Field, Clearwater

☞ Pittsburgh Pirates: McKechnie Field, Bradenton

☞ St. Louis Cardinals: Roger Dean Stadium, Jupiter

☞ Tampa Bay Devil Rays: Progress Energy Field, Home of Al Lang Field, St. Petersburg

☞ Toronto Blue Jays: Knology Park, Dunedin

☞ Washington Nationals: Space Coast Stadium, Viera

Florida's Speed Zone

Daytona International Speedway is also known as the "World Center of Racing" and the "Home of Speed." The track is the home of the Daytona 500, known as the "Great American Race." And speed is not just for race day—because of the track's incredibly steep curves, cars must be going at least 60 miles per hour, or they risk falling off the track!

DID YOU KNOW?

☞ Florida is home to more than 1250 golf courses—more than any other state. And Palm Beach County has more golf courses than any other U.S. county.

☞ Fort Lauderdale is the site of the International Swimming Hall of Fame, which spotlights the world's best swimmers.

- Coral Gables is the home of the largest swimming pool in the continental U.S.

- The Pinellas Trail, a 47-mile hiking/biking trail, is the longest urban linear trail in the eastern U.S.

A Sure Bet

Horse racing is legal in South Florida, and a growing number of horse racetracks are available, including Calder Race Course in Miami Gardens, Gulfstream Park in Hallandale, Hialeah Park, Pompano Park and Tampa Bay Downs. The state takes pride in its thoroughbred industry. All told, Florida has produced 41 North American champions, 86 equine millionaires, 18 Breeder Cup winners and 19 Classic winners, including 1978 Triple Crown–winner, Affirmed.

 Dog racing is legal in North Florida, and the Sunshine State has more dog racetracks than any other state.

Home of the "World's Fastest Game"

Professional jai alai in the United States got its start in Miami, and both the city and the state have truly embraced this lightning-quick sport.

- There are more jai alai frontons (arenas) in Florida than in any other place in the world.

- Miami is home to the nation's oldest jai alai fronton.

- Jai alai really is the world's fastest ball game (as the slogan states). The nearly baseball-sized *pelota* has been clocked at speeds over 180 miles per hour.

☛ The game that developed into modern-day jai alai is more than 300 years old, but it has only been in the United States—and Florida—for a little over 80 years.

☛ Jai alai was introduced as a professional game at the Miami Fronton in 1926.

☛ The game originated in the Basque region of the Pyrenees Mountains. *Jai alai* means "merry festival" in Basque.

TALL TALES, URBAN LEGENDS AND STRANGE SITUATIONS

Beware the Skunk Ape

Throughout the history of Florida, a growing number of witnesses have reported encounters with what may be the state's most famous myth. Known as the "Skunk Ape," the creature is believed to be similar to the Sasquatch or Bigfoot in the northwestern United States.

Described as a hairy ape-man standing seven to eight feet tall and weighing 300 to 600 pounds, the creature's most memorable characteristic is its particularly funky odor, which is said to smell like a blend of skunk, cow manure and rotting eggs and cabbage. The prevailing theory about the odor's source, as well as why a real-life Skunk Ape has never been caught or shot, is that the creature is said to make its home in unoccupied underground alligator nests within the state's swampland, especially in the Everglades, and its hairy body absorbs a lot of stinky methane gas. However, others believe that the creature(s) may dwell in North Florida, in order to escape repeated hurricanes.

For more than 200 years, the Skunk Ape, also known as the "Swamp Monkey" and the "Bardin Booger" or "Boogie Man," has appeared in the folklore of both Florida's pioneers and the native inhabitants. Florida's Seminole people have long had legends of these giant man-beasts, which they referred to as the "Sand People" and the "Mangrove People." Meanwhile, scientific researchers believe that the Skunk Ape—if he/she/it actually exists—may be the descendent of an unknown primate.

The greatest wave of sightings occurred in the 1970s, with all reports providing the same description of the creature. And while the number of reports decreased in following decades, they really picked up in the new millennium, as Florida's wilderness rapidly makes way for development. In all, about 75 sightings, complete with photos and videos, have been reported statewide over the past 20 years. In fact, the number of Skunk Ape sightings ranks second for Bigfoot-type sightings, after the Pacific Northwest (the home of Sasquatch).

The best evidence for the Skunk Ape's existence may have been provided in late 2000, when the Sarasota County Sheriff's office received several photographs and a letter from an anonymous source. The Myakka Skunk Ape photographs, as they were referred to, clearly showed a large, orangutan-like creature with visible details of forehead lines, yellow canines, fingernails and hair. The letter's writer claimed that the creature had repeatedly entered their yard to steal apples from a basket on the porch.

In another encounter, a young couple making out in their truck was startled by a huge, smelly creature that shook their vehicle, causing the wheels to come off the ground. The couple managed to escape on foot and reported their encounter.

In 2004, a woman driving on a rural South Florida road at sundown spotted what she thought was a large animal crouched in a ditch. Upon closer scrutiny, the woman realized that the creature looked different from anything she'd ever seen; her description matched the many others.

One reported encounter has been proven false, even by dedicated fans. The case involved a Skunk Ape that was captured alive by the U.S. Army and held in a secret concrete vault at Everglades National Park. The creature was said to have escaped into the wild. Regardless of whether the other reports are true, the Skunk Ape has become a beloved part of Florida folklore.

For the Birds

The year 1948 was a great one for giant bird sightings! First, witnesses reported seeing a 15-foot-tall penguin that left big tracks along the shore of Clearwater Beach. Another giant penguin-like bird was seen floating on the water by tourists on a boat off the Gulf. Still another big, penguin-like bird was spotted by a private airplane pilot on the banks of North Florida's Suwannee River.

Look Out Below!

Here is a selection of firsthand accounts of strange materials dive-bombing from out of the clouds.

- ☛ In February 1958, a glittering, mysterious glob fell from the clouds over Miami, where it dissolved immediately, leaving no traces.

- ☛ In May 1959, a frozen hen's egg plummeted to the ground in Orlando.

- ☛ On September 3, 1969, hundreds of golf balls crashed down in Punta Gorda.

- ☛ In September 1971, thousands of fish rained down on Port Richey.

- ☛ In September 1978, Lake Worth residents were bombarded by actual ice cubes falling from the sky.

Great Balls of Fire

In Florida, there have been three reported cases of spontaneous human combustion (SHC). First, in Jacksonville on October 9, 1980, Jeanna Winchester, a naval airwoman, burst into flames while sitting in a car with her friend. The friend tried to put out the flames, but the car crashed into a telephone pole. Winchester was rushed to the hospital and survived, but 20 percent of her body, including her right shoulder and arm, neck, side and back, was burned. The police investigated but found no cause.

Then, in Tampa, in the early 1950s, Mary Reeser's case of SHC yielded a huge amount of investigation, but no explanation was ever found. Finally, in Miami in 1975, Ethal Cooks reportedly burst into flame; her body was totally consumed by the high heat, but the surrounding areas—even the chair she'd been sitting in—were hardly touched by the fire!